ROSA'S CHILD

ROSA'S CHILD

*The True Story of One Woman's
Quest for a Lost Mother and a
Vanished Past*

JEREMY JOSEPHS

with

Susi Bechhöfer

I.B. Tauris Publishers
LONDON · NEW YORK

Reprinted in 1999 by I.B.Tauris & Co Ltd
Victoria House, Bloomsbury Square, London WC1B 4DZ
175 Fifth Avenue, New York NY 10010

In the United States and Canada distributed by St. Martin's Press
175 Fifth Avenue, New York NY 10010

First published in 1996 by I.B.Tauris & Co Ltd

ISBN 1 86064 122 9

A full CIP record for this book is available from the British Library
A full CIP record for this book is available from the Library of Congress

Library of Congress catalog card: available

Typeset in Monotype Ehrhardt by Lucy Morton, London
Printed and bound in Great Britain by WBC Ltd, Bridgend

Contents

PART II   Towards the Light

For Rosa

Author's Preface

It can hardly be described as perfect timing. For I only heard of Susi Bechhöfer's story a few weeks before I was due to leave England with a view to settling in France. But as soon as a few details of her biography were described to me I was immediately hooked and wanted to find out more. Interested in both the Holocaust – which provides a shadowy background to the Bechhöfer case – and human psychology, I knew right away that Susi's tragic but ultimately uplifting story had to be the subject of my next book.

I was fortunate that Susi was equally anxious for her story to be told. The upshot was that Susi and I agreed from the start that we would pull no punches in telling her story, however unpalatable some of the facts might be. I must therefore put on record my deep appreciation of Susi's frank and open approach to the many hours of interviews to which I subjected her. Throughout our sessions I was all too aware of the pain that my constant prodding at unhappy memories was causing her, and yet she never lost sight of the fact that her efforts were in a good cause, and perhaps essential for her peace of mind.

In my view this is one of the most unusual of the many harrowing stories that have their roots in the Holocaust years, and I only hope that I have done justice to both its complexity and its sheer horror. One thing I am certain of is that its telling would have been far less easy without the skilful editing of Richard Dawes and the productive help from the staff at I.B. Tauris.

I should also like to express my gratitude to Cynthia Anton, Edward and Irene Mann, Frederick Stocken, Alan Stocken, Jerry Bechhofer, Bertha Leverton, Clare Fay, Lucy Morton, Edith Moses, Mavis and James Wainman, Sally George and, of course, Susi Bechhöfer herself, whose determination to confront her past and bear the burden of what she found is surely an inspiration to us all.

Jeremy Josephs,
Montpellier, France, 1996

PART I
In the Shadows

ONE

Forbidden by Decree

Rosa Bechhöfer had little cause to complain. Compared with the plight of many of the Jews of Fürth, she was positively well off. In the two years since Hitler had assumed power, the Bavarian city's Jewish community had been reeling from a string of harsh discriminatory decrees. First they had been barred from holding public office or working for the civil service. Then journalism, teaching, farming and the arts had become out of bounds. Perhaps one day Rosa's more modest employ might also be proscribed by law. But so far, her job as a sales assistant in her sister Frieda's shoe shop in the city centre had evaded the lawmakers' net.

Rosa complained all the same, although her unhappiness had nothing to do with the employment laws: it was simply that marriage had eluded her. Eligible Jewish men tended to seek out the daughters of wealthy families: with her thirty-seventh birthday not far off, and not a penny to her name, Rosa's chances of ever standing proudly beneath the *chuppah*, the Jewish wedding canopy, were looking increasingly slim. She wondered if she might fare better in the more cosmopolitan Bavarian capital, Munich, a ninety-minute train ride to the south.

If Rosa showed some reluctance to leave Fürth, it was under-

3

standable, for she had lived and worked in the historic city for more than thirty years, and it was the only home she knew. Although her parents, Sara and Gabriel Bechhöfer, had had thirteen children, of whom Rosa was number twelve, she had never basked in the warmth of family life – at least not for long. Her parents both passed away when she was six, and from that age, together with the youngest child, Betty, she had been brought up in Fürth's squalid municipal orphanage.

By the end of February 1935 Rosa had made up her mind to leave Fürth, having secured a job in Munich as a domestic servant with the well-to-do Kreschower family. But scarcely had she settled into her new routine than she was forced to begin looking for another position. Jews who could afford to leave Munich, or bid farewell to Germany itself, were deserting the city, and the Kreschowers had managed to obtain the documentation necessary to emigrate to the USA.

Ironically, Rosa had been working for only eight weeks for her next employers, the Grünbaums, in their well-appointed house in Kaulbachstrasse, when they too packed their bags and left Germany for good. This time, though, Rosa had herself managed to move rapidly. The very next day, 1 September 1935, she took up her third position, with the Levingers at 6 Rosenstrasse. She prayed, in those unsettling times, that she might at least be more secure in her employment.

But stability was not the lot of Germany's Jews during the 1930s. Rosa had been in her new job barely a fortnight when she learned that she was to be stripped of her German citizenship. Nor was she alone in this, for she shared her fate with every single one of Germany's Jews. Over a decade earlier, Hitler had conceived two far-reaching legal instruments, both now unanimously approved at a convention of the Nazi Party in Nuremberg. The Law of the Reich Citizen could hardly have been more explicit. In short, the Jews of Germany were no longer full citizens but mere subjects of the state.

And if, in her quest for a happily married life, Rosa had as much as contemplated wedding a man from outside of her own faith, such a notion was dispelled from her mind by the Law for the Protection of German Blood and German Honour. This legislation, which came into force with the Law of the Reich Citizen, explicitly forbade marriages between Jews and Aryans, as well as extramarital relationships between them. This law in particular reflected a key element in National Socialist thinking: under no circumstances whatever should Jewish blood be allowed to taint Aryans.

Yet Rosa Bechhöfer surely had as good a claim to citizenship as any Aryan in the Fatherland. She could trace her roots back to the middle of the sixteenth century, when her seven-times great-grandfather was born. Not many Germans could point to such a pedigree. Rosa's distant forebear had been born and bred in Bechhofen, some thirty miles southwest of Fürth, and the ancient Bavarian village, with its famous synagogue and medieval cemetery, was where Rosa had spent the first six years of her life.

For centuries the Jews of Bavaria had no family names. Only in 1815 did surnames come to be required by law. Thus it was that, two years before this deadline, a certain Josef Ber, Rosa's great-great-grandfather, set about choosing a name for the family. What could be better than Bechhöfer, he thought, to denote people born and raised in Bechhofen.

Rosa's lineage nevertheless failed to impress the upholders of the Nuremberg Laws. From their perspective, the entire Bechhöfer clan could have been resident in the same area since the primeval mists – it made not the slightest difference. Try as they might, they would never be deemed worthy of regaining the status of citizens of the German state. The reason was perfectly simple: the Bechhöfers were, and always would be, Jews. As if this was not enough, in time over a dozen additional decrees would outlaw Rosa and her race completely.

5

The blood circulating in the veins of Joseph Otto Hald suffered from no such shortcomings. Aryan through and through, it even had a touch of German nobility not so far in the past. For all that, Otto Hald did not boast the piercing blue eyes and blond hair of the Nazis' stereotype Aryan. He was slim, lean and dark-haired, with sparkling brown eyes. Twenty-eight years old and a welder by trade, Otto had been forced to abandon his work to serve in the German army, whose expansionary ambitions were belatedly beginning to sound alarm bells in London and Paris. Otto's heart was not in it, however, and in his case his rank of private reflected a total lack of commitment to the imperial vision of the Führer.

Born near Stuttgart, like Rosa he had travelled to Munich to improve his fortunes. His dream was that one day he would patent and then sell the welding substance he had devised. But the advent of Hitler and the relentless militarization of Germany had thwarted his plans. Unlike Rosa, however, whose lodgings consisted of a single room up an old stone spiral staircase above a chemist's shop, Otto Hald was living in some style. There was money in the family, especially on his mother's side, the von Eiffs. His elegant flat was situated just a stone's throw from that chemist's shop, on the other side of Munich's oldest church, the Peterskirche, built in the twelfth century.

The handsome soldier had deliberately chosen the old part of Munich. In part it was because of the charm conferred on the district by its wealth of fine baroque and rococo architecture. But more importantly, it seemed to Otto that this bustling city was the ideal place to pursue his two great passions: the seduction of women and the consumption of alcohol. A highly eligible bachelor, Otto knew that many women were attracted by his dark good looks and carefree manner. It was an arrangement that suited him well, for their feelings were more often than not reciprocated with great enthusiasm. Otto was, and would remain for the rest of his life, a perfect example of a ladies' man.

As the delegates to the 1935 National Socialist convention at Nuremberg began to disperse from the city, satisfied with the drafting of the Gesetz zum Schutze des Deutschen Blutes und der Deutschen Ehre, the decree which outlawed liaisons of any kind between Jews and 'citizens of German or kindred blood', Rosa Bechhöfer was confronted with a harsh biological fact. She was pregnant. And though she did not yet know it, she was carrying twins. As he was about to find out, the father was Otto Hald, he of the irrefutably German or kindred blood.

Little is known of Rosa and Otto's relationship. It may have been a passionate love affair that they were determined should flourish despite the prevailing intolerance, now sanctioned by law. Or perhaps it was just a one-night stand. Hard facts are in short supply, perhaps because, after all, they were anxious not to fly in the face of Nazi prejudice. Maybe Otto had some connection with the Kreschowers, the Grünbaums or the Levingers, Rosa's employers. Or perhaps Rosa and Otto had simply found themselves sitting next to each other in one of the many bustling beer-houses near where they lived and a casual conversation sparked off the chemistry of mutual desire. But in truth, how these two strangers, whose backgrounds could scarcely have been more different, became involved with each other, remains a mystery.

What is not a matter of speculation, however, is the ominous clarification provided on 14 November 1935 by the first supplementary decree of the Nuremberg Laws. This defined precisely what a Jew was. A Jew was a person with at least one Jewish grandparent. Further legislation was intended to complete the process of segregation, with Jews now forbidden to 'employ in domestic service female subjects of German or kindred blood who are under the age of 45 years'. Before long Jewish passports were being stamped with a yellow 'J' for 'Jude' and Jews were compelled to adopt Jewish names, so as to be more easily identified.

None of this was of much concern to Rosa Bechhöfer, who had never denied her Jewishness. Both her grandparents were Jewish, as had been their grandparents before them, and all of them were strictly orthodox. Admittedly she had yet to acquire a passport upon which some zealous official could then stamp his large golden gothic lettering, but unsurprisingly she was more worried about developments going on inside her own body. Her employers, the Levingers, pledged that, if she wished, she could continue to work for them until the very end of her confinement. They were prepared to stand by her. However, of much greater concern to Rosa was whether Otto would do likewise.

He did not. By the time Rosa was halfway through her pregnancy, in February 1936, Otto had gone. He too knew all about the consequences of flouting the Nuremberg decrees. Jews and Aryans discovered to be in relationships with each other were already being sent to concentration camps. The camp at Dachau, the first to be built in Germany, just five weeks after Hitler had become Chancellor in January 1933, was rather too close for comfort, being only some twelve miles north of Munich. Otto Hald had no intention of joining its growing number of inmates.

Otto's flight from Munich left Rosa in a predicament. Part of her was happy to have at last conceived. For many years she had hoped one day to bear a child of her own, longing to be a mother rather than an aunt. But the circumstances of her pregnancy were hardly what she had had in mind. Naturally she wondered if her large, if somewhat dispersed, family might now break with their past behaviour and show compassion towards her. They did not. The depressing truth was that most of the Bechhöfer siblings who remained in Germany viewed their errant sister's condition with dismay.

As soon as they were old enough to understand, the message had been drummed into them that for a man and a woman to produce a child out of wedlock was a violation of Mosaic law. The teachings of the Jewish scriptures had been spurned. And when, inevitably, they discovered that the father was not only a Gentile but a serving member of the army of Adolf Hitler, there was precious little sympathy on offer.

Hermann Bechhöfer, the third born, was particularly disgusted. At long last he was on the point of being granted the various visas he needed to set off to America. It had been a complicated process which had taken up a great deal of time and energy. Might there not be consequences for Hermann and his wife Jenny if the authorities learned that the strict laws concerning racial purity had been so flagrantly violated in his own family?

Among the Bechhöfers, Rosa's pregnancy soon became a taboo subject, something shameful only to be whispered about behind closed doors. For orthodox Jews from Fürth it was nothing less than a blot on the family name, and a potentially dangerous blot at that. Not for the first time in her life, Rosa found herself alone.

Or almost alone. Only her sister, Frieda Behr, in whose shoe shop Rosa had worked before leaving Fürth, showed genuine concern. A married woman without children, Frieda decided that the most practical help she could give her younger sister was financial. And she was right, for Rosa's meagre wage as a domestic servant barely covered her living expenses. Even though Rosa had not made contact with Munich's Jewish community since arriving there, Frieda suggested that she should consider giving birth in the city's Jewish hospital, a private, fee-paying institution – Frieda would meet all the costs. Rosa gratefully accepted.

Sensing that the twins might arrive prematurely, Rosa decided on a course of action that she hoped would herald a new beginning. Her employers, the Levingers, were in the process of applying to emigrate to the USA. Seeing the writing on the wall, Rosa's brother Isaak had done the same within a year of Hitler's accession to power in 1933. Now Rosa decided to follow their example. With the Levingers' permission she dashed around Munich, from one office to another, in an urgent attempt to gather together all the papers she needed before the twins arrived.

Rosa was well aware that her chances of success would be much better if Isaak and his wife Martha, now both American citizens, would swear an affidavit endorsing her application. She also knew that the USA, only just emerging from the Depression, could ill afford to receive refugees destined to become a burden on the economy, however deserving their case. Rosa wrote letters to her family in New York pleading for an affidavit. Isaak Bechhöfer contacted his cousin, Julius Selling, the only well-to-do member of the family in the USA. Selling promised he would 'do something'. But, despite several visits by Isaak and his daughter Senta, Julius Selling never kept his promise. Isaak was in no position to provide an affidavit: he lacked the necessary assets.

Whether an affidavit would have smoothed the way for Rosa is a matter of conjecture. To obtain a visa to enter the USA a person needed to be registered at the US Consulate in Stuttgart and receive a 'quota number'. Unfortunately, many people's numbers were never reached before they were deported by the Nazis. There is no knowledge of Rosa's quota number. Had it been a low one, and had Julius Selling sent an affidavit, she and her children might have been given the coveted visa.

On 17 May 1936 Rosa went into labour. Before the day was over she had given birth to two girls: Lotte and Susi. In the eyes of their proud mother, Lotte was the spitting image of her father, while Susi had the unmistakably Semitic looks of Rosa herself. Lotte was dark, alert and had bright eyes; Susi's eyes seemed to reflect the sadness that Rosa felt in her heart.

Within the twins' first few days a number of events occurred which were to have a profound impact on the course of their lives. First, Rosa learned that the Levingers had been granted permission to settle in the USA. That came as no surprise, but she herself was to have no such luck, for she soon received formal notification that her application had not been successful. Worse, it had not even received serious consideration. At a stroke, all her hopes of starting a new life in America with her two daughters had been shattered.

The bureaucrats of the immigration authorities in New York had had no interest in an unmarried and pregnant, penniless and unskilled refugee whose own relatives were not prepared to stand as guarantors. Their refusal obliged Rosa to find another job in domestic service, and in this at least she was successful. Less than three months after giving birth, Rosa was back at work tending to the domestic affairs of middle-class Munich Jews. As she went about her daily chores only one question preoccupied her: whatever was to become of Lotte and Susi, still slightly jaundiced as they lay in their cots at the Jewish hospital?

Sometime during the late summer of 1936 a formidable figure wearing a nurse's starched white apron and cap pulled up in a taxi outside that building and asked the driver to wait for her. Not long afterwards she re-emerged with Susi tucked securely under one arm, Lotte under the other. Alice Bendix, the visitor to the hospital, was the efficient and highly respected matron of the Antonienheim, named after the quiet Antonienstrasse in which it was situated. Others called it the Kinderheim – the Children's Home – but however it was referred to the fact remained that it was Munich's Jewish orphanage.

Before leaving for the hospital Alice Bendix had told children and staff alike that they should prepare to give a warm welcome to two very special guests. At the orphanage there was great excitement and anticipation as the children tried to guess what the matron had meant. When she later returned with Susi and Lotte, no one was disappointed. The twins were received as honoured newcomers, and every person in the building made their way down to the nursery to greet them. What none of those one hundred or so ardent admirers could have known was that the Bechhöfer twins would not take a single step outside their new home until one day before their third birthday. Or indeed that when that day came, they would walk away without the hand of their mother or father there to guide them on the long journey ahead.

From the start it was Lotte who stole the hearts of everyone. Slightly bigger than her sister, she had a round, chubby face and a cheerful and outgoing nature. She was full of affection, constantly wanting to be picked up and cuddled. Susi, tiny and fairer of colouring, made no attempt to reach out to people. Instead, two large brown eyes, in a dainty, fragile face, seemed to look out on the world with a rather serious curiosity. She cried a great deal, sometimes uncontrollably. No one said as much, but little Lotte was unquestionably most people's favourite. And yet perhaps Susi's more cautious outlook stood her in good stead for what life was later to bring.

Antonienstrasse was a short, mostly residential street close to the celebrated English Gardens. The home was at number seven, a large building which seemed to be bulging with a surfeit of balconies. Surrounding the orphanage was a well-tended garden, which, although it had only a small lawn, was dotted with many mature fruit trees and bushes that sprouted dozens of kinds of berries. The dining rooms and playrooms were situated downstairs, while upstairs the bedrooms were painted in different colours: greens, blues and yellows predominating. The nursery, where the twins had found themselves together with three other little souls, was a spacious room painted bright pink. Just along the corridor were the bathrooms, with rows of small sinks, tiny toilets and miniature bath-tubs.

Although food was sometimes in short supply – often there was no breakfast and lunch the same day might be of limited nutritional value – the atmosphere in the Antonienheim was invariably pleasant. By contrast, the political framework in which it functioned was becoming more and more sinister with each passing day. And unbeknown to Alice Bendix, the legal status of the orphanage was about to be reviewed.

Responsibility for the care of the twins passed to Helene Pressburger, a qualified nursery nurse from Stuttgart and one of the most popular personalities working in the Antonienheim. But in practice day-to-day care of the babies in her charge fell to the older children, who were appointed as carers. The policy was entirely pragmatic, for scarce resources demanded that the older children take care of the little ones. This was how eleven-year-old Ruth Bruckner and her brother Walter came to be responsible for Lotte and Susi. They made an excellent job of preparing the twins' food, lovingly feeding and bathing them, and taking care of their considerable laundry requirements.

Rosa would have dearly loved to perform all these tasks for them, but circumstances prevented her doing so. It seemed to be her destiny to tend to the needs of others rather than those of her own children. She felt enormously guilty about it, and to compound her self-condemnation there was the unspoken but almost unanimous disapproval of her family to contend with. Rosa visited the Antonienheim regularly. She would appear nearly every Sunday, her day off, arriving soon after the twins had finished their lunch. Delighted though she was to spend precious time with her daughters, her visits never failed to cause her great pain.

To Edith Moses, one of the orphanage's many volunteer teachers, Rosa's grief was all too plain to see. 'It was the same story every week when it came to saying goodbye to the twins. She could hardly bring herself to look at them because she used to get so upset. That's why she was always to be seen rushing away from the building.'

The only other Bechhöfer to visit the Antonienheim was Frieda, who made it her business to drop in from time to time. Her view of her nieces clearly accorded with what others said of them, for on the back of one of the photographs she took at the orphanage she wrote: 'Lotte – an angel', while on the front was the revealing inscription: 'Susi – rather difficult'.

By the time the girls had moved from the nursery into the kindergarten, at the age of eighteen months, their mother had changed addresses three more times. The pattern was familiar to her: the Jews of Munich with sufficient funds or foresight were on the move. Seeing them secure their families' future, Rosa decided on a change of plan for her own children. If she could not emigrate, might it not be possible to evacuate them? She asked Alice Bendix what could be done.

Despite the ever-increasing tension for the city's Jews, the head of the Antonienheim had remained adamant. On Friday nights strict observance of Jewish traditions would continue: candles would be lit, Kaddish recited and ancient Hebrew songs sung. This atmosphere, intended to recreate historic Jewish family life and following customs handed down over the centuries, was readily absorbed by the twins. Indeed the heralding in of the Sabbath was a ritual to which everyone in the orphanage, children and staff alike, looked forward eagerly. For they knew that after the completion of prayers a wholesome meal of fried fish and potato salad awaited them.

The Kristallnacht of 9 November 1938 obliged Alice Bendix to amend these practices. Now there could be no doubting that the Jews of Germany were in grave danger. The 'Night of Broken Glass' spread horror throughout the country's Jewry, wanton destruction and violence on a national scale having replaced legal coercion. A Nazi Party internal report prepared the following day contained the first grim statistics:

> The extent of the destruction of Jewish shops and houses cannot yet be verified by figures. Eight hundred and fifteen shops destroyed, 171 dwelling houses set on fire, only indicate a fraction of the damage so far as arson is concerned. One hundred and nineteen synagogues were set on fire, another 76 completely destroyed. Twenty thousand Jews were arrested. Thirty-six deaths were reported and those seriously injured also numbered 36. All those killed and injured are Jews.

The final tally of murder and destruction throughout the country was much higher: about one hundred Jews killed and three hundred synagogues burned down. In addition some 30,000 Jews had been arrested and a number of cases of rape had been reported. The twisted logic of the Nazis led them to regard rape in these circumstances as more reprehensible than murder, since it violated the Nuremberg decrees forbidding sexual relations between Gentiles and Jews.

A few days later the Jewish communities of Germany were informed that they must pay for the destruction of their own property. For good measure, a collective fine was imposed on them of one billion Reichmarks. And all this at the orders of their own government.

In Munich tension was running at fever pitch. Desperate to renew her plea on behalf of the twins, Rosa returned to the Antonienheim. Aware that there was now talk in the city of transportations being organized to evacuate Jewish children from Germany, she begged for two places to be found for hers. Alice Bendix had already taken the initiative, and now informed Rosa that she had contacted various Jewish organizations in the USA and had apparently obtained clearance for the twins to be adopted by a wealthy orthodox

Jewish family in California. She had even recruited a twenty-year-old Jewish woman, Hannah Bronstein, to spend time at the orphanage acquainting herself with the sisters, now sprightly toddlers of two-and-a-half. As soon as the twins felt comfortable with her she would accompany them on the long and arduous journey to America's West Coast. The formalities were about to be finalized.

Rosa was taken aback by the plan. But in the aftermath of Kristallnacht, and with Lotte and Susi's welfare her greatest priority, she knew that Alice Bendix's arrangements were probably the best she could hope for.

Just a couple of miles away members of the Nazi Party were completing the preparations for a massive celebration of Aryan art. Almost the entire Nazi leadership was to gather there, with the proceedings culminating in a pageant of knights in armour and flaxen-haired Rhinemaidens to symbolize their conception of two thousand years of Germanic culture. As they did so, Alice Bendix was putting the finishing touches to her own project – and not just on behalf of the Bechhöfer twins, for she was battling to dispatch overseas every one of the children who remained in her care. True, after Kristallnacht progress had become a little faster. But there were still official procedures to be followed, with the inevitable delays that these entail. And then suddenly, on the morning of 16 May 1939, there was a sense of urgency in the air. In the Antonienheim little suitcases were being packed.

Ruth Bruckner recalls that day vividly. She noticed that the twins were gone, but had no idea where. Nor could she get any answer beyond: 'They've gone'. By the time the young girl asked about the whereabouts of her charges, they were already out of the country.

TWO

Grace and Eunice

Irene Mann was ironing in her kitchen one day in November 1938 when suddenly her husband came in clutching the *Daily Telegraph*. After attending to some business in the centre of Cardiff, he had been reading the paper while drinking a coffee in the Kardomah café. Now, in his warm but firm voice, he read his wife part of an article which said that, as a result of the situation in Germany, thousands of refugee children desperately needed a home. The newspaper invited readers to take such a child into their care; when her husband asked if she would be willing to do so, Irene, always eager to comply with his wishes, agreed enthusiastically.

Before long the couple – 28-year-old Edward Mann, a Baptist minister, and his wife Irene, four years his senior and likewise a devout Christian – had made contact with the German Jewish Aid Committee in London, and there began six months of correspondence in preparation for their fostering of a Jewish child.

Many newspapers had carried reports similar to the one the Reverend Mann had read out to his wife. For it was the period just after Kristallnacht, and world opinion had been appalled by the deeds of a nation which, while possessing an ancient culture combining Christianity and humanism, had nevertheless acted with shocking barbarity. And nowhere had this outrage been expressed more eloquently than in the British press. Now it was clear: the Third Reich was going down a dark path from which there was to be no return.

The savagery of Kristallnacht had finally propelled the British government into addressing the refugee question. The Home Secretary, Sir Samuel Hoare, announced that with immediate effect visas and passports for refugee children from Europe would no longer be necessary. All that would be required now was a single travel document. At last the large-scale exodus of young people from Germany and Austria, for which Jewish organizations in Britain had been campaigning vigorously, could take place. During the months leading up to the outbreak of the Second World War in September 1939, nearly 10,000 children, most but by no means all Jewish, were to be delivered from Nazi oppression to safety in Britain. They were the Kindertransport children.

Eventually the Manns were offered a child, but when they learned that she would be coming with her mother they wrote to the German Jewish Aid Committee to explain that they would prefer to care for a refugee who had no one to look after him or her. The committee then asked them to consider taking two little girls from an orphanage in Munich who were in great need of care. At once Irene was concerned about the extra cost, so the couple wrote to say they would be happy to consider taking one of the girls, whose names, they had been told, were Susi and Lotte Bechhöfer.

When the Manns received a photograph of the sisters it confirmed Irene's suspicion that they were twins. But now, on seeing them, instead of rejecting the idea out of hand she turned to her husband and asked him to decide. Neither felt that they should separate the girls, and after much heart-searching, they wrote to say that they would, after all, take both of them.

As this correspondence continued, what the Manns did

not know was that the Central British Fund, responsible for providing most of the finance for the Kindertransport, was desperately short of money. With the Fund overwhelmed by demand and insolvency fast approaching, Earl Baldwin, the former Prime Minister Stanley Baldwin, took to the airwaves to see if his authority might assist in some way. Through the good offices of the BBC, he called upon the British people to rally to the aid of the victims of a catastrophe. 'It is not an earthquake, nor a flood or a famine,' he explained, 'but an explosion of man's inhumanity to man.'

The public responded generously, donating over half a million pounds to the Central British Fund. So popular was the broadcast that it became something of a hit when it was distributed on record at eight shillings a disc, bringing in yet more money. Much of the total revenue was allocated to the cost of maintaining the refugees, a figure which the German Jewish Aid Committee managed to pare down to just under one pound per child per week.

The new flexibility being shown by the British government did not mean that all bureaucratic procedures had been cast aside. Documents still had to be processed in large numbers. Once dealt with in London, applications to leave Germany were sent back to the Reich. There, some of these forms would simply be rejected by the German or Austrian police and the word 'unacceptable' stamped in large black letters across the documents – usually for no apparent reason. In each such case, the fate of a child had been sealed at a stroke.

The German Jewish Aid Committee was almost overwhelmed by the enormity of the task it faced. One thousand children were setting off every month, with an average of two transports departing from various European capitals each week. Nor was demand slowing. On the contrary, as war grew ever more inevitable, more and more parents became anxious to evacuate their children. Five thousand letters were

arriving every week at the organization's London head-
quarters, where the atmosphere was one of near chaos. It
was even worse in Germany and Austria, where preparations
for departure were almost always made at the last minute,
with selection for inclusion in a particular transportation
being a haphazard affair.

And yet, despite these great odds, the general secretary of
the Refugee Children's Movement would later affirm: 'It is
not a small thing in these years of suffering without parallel,
to have given to ten thousand children the opportunity to
grow up in an atmosphere of decency and normality, to work,
to play, to laugh and be happy and to assume their rightful
heritage as free men and women.' But were the Bechhöfer
twins, who were soon to arrive in England, destined to find
themselves in such an environment?

As committee members combed through the papers from
prospective foster families, they were briefed to look out for
upper-middle-class Jewish parents, preferably professional
people who already had children of their own. Ideally they
would live in the country, away from the enticements of
urban life. And if, in addition, they spoke fluent German,
then they immediately qualified as perfect foster parents and
were recruited without delay.

Naturally, few applicants met these requirements, and
whatever their other virtues, the Reverend and Irene Mann
certainly did not. They were from the lower middle classes.
Their home could hardly be described as being in the
countryside, for it was a stone's throw from the centre of
Cardiff. Nor, much to their regret, did they have children.
As for speaking German, they could not put together a
sentence between them. And crucially, not only were they
not Jews, but Edward Mann was a Baptist of the non-
conformist, fundamentalist tendency, whose reputation was
growing all the time, both as a teacher of the New Testament
and as a stirring preacher of the Gospel. However, there

were not enough Jews coming forward as prospective foster parents, and so, despite all these apparent disqualifications, to their great joy the couple were accepted.

'My husband detests the Victorian era,' Irene Mann had a habit of saying, 'but he would have done very well in it all the same.' She was right. Edward Mann had grown up in and still inhabited an enclosed, ordered world of religious devotion, his every move revolving around his role as a minister. It was a busy life, for among other duties he was obliged to deliver two lengthy sermons every Sunday. This duty he would carry out with panache, gesticulating expressively from the pulpit with his arms. Then there were Bible studies to conduct, meetings to chair, and, with Irene, the counselling of members of his congregation whenever the need arose.

Although he undoubtedly believed in the scriptures, the Reverend Mann understood little of the Christian concept of humility. Instead he was a powerful, dominant and, to the many people who came under his spell, charismatic man. What Edward Mann wanted, he usually got.

There was one notable exception to this rule, however. For some years he and his wife had been trying without success for a child. In fact Edward Mann was so frustrated by his lack of paternity that it came to haunt him daily throughout his life. Indeed, in time he would find himself virtually incapable of conducting a service of dedication to bless a newborn baby. Obsessed by their childlessness, he often came close to shaking his fist at God. Therefore it is not surprising that, although there was often warmth and laughter in the home, there was a permanent undercurrent of friction within the marriage. The gifted Bible teacher was angry. In his view his wife ought to have borne him a son. Had she not therefore singularly failed in her duty to him?

This was the home in which the Bechhöfer girls were to spend their formative years. The plan conceived by Alice

Bendix for them to settle in California had fallen through at the last minute. Even so, the twins could count themselves among the lucky ones, for two places had been found for them on a Kindertransport to London instead. The same could not be said for the twenty or so other children from the Antonienheim, who never succeeded in crossing the German border. The bold slogan of the hour had been 'Save the Children'. The charity bearing that name was involved in what had become a desperate, last-ditch relief operation. Despite all the good work, not all the children were to be saved.

On 18 May 1939 the train carrying Susi and Lotte Bechhöfer pulled into London's Liverpool Street station. It had been a 36-hour journey for the twins, who, the previous day, had spent their third birthday on a Kindertransport. Wearing identity labels around their necks and each clutching a small suitcase in one hand and a cuddly toy in the other, the bewildered little girls emerged onto the platform of the huge rail terminus. A voluntary worker in Munich had gone to some trouble to explain to them that they were leaving the orphanage to go on a long and very special journey – something that neither of them had ever done before. If this was meant to furnish a full explanation of why they were now in a strange place where everyone spoke a strange language, it had evidently not done the trick.

Within minutes of leaving the train, Susi and Lotte were to be seen walking off in obvious distress, a pitiful sight as they struggled with their luggage, determined to hang on to each other's hands as they did so. Ushered along by the good women of the children's refugee committee, they were in tears as they slowly made their way to a large, dimly lit room. There, women clutching clipboards and calling out surnames which sometimes they struggled to pronounce, were busy processing the 160 new arrivals.

The refugee committee had set up shop in an enclosed

space by a taxi ramp at one end of the station. On one side were seats and benches for those children destined for hostels and camps. The other side had been designated for children already allocated foster parents, and it was here that Susi and Lotte were told to sit, although they did not know why.

'There I found these two children, little tots, having been lifted up onto the seat, with their legs dangling,' recalls Irene Mann, who had travelled up from Cardiff to meet the twins from the train. The Reverend Mann had been unable to accompany her because he was conducting an important funeral that day.

> They looked very dazed and very bemused, wondering where they were. They were not dressed alike. They weren't looking as if they were identical twins. It must have all been very strange for them, wondering what had happened to them. So I held out my hands to them and I said: 'Come.' '*Nein*,' they said, and shook their heads. So, I thought, that's a fine start. So I went back to the lady in charge and I said: 'Would you come with me and speak to them? Put them at ease. Tell them what I'm about to do.' And Lotte said to her: 'Are we going home?' To which the lady replied: 'If you take the hand of this lady here, she is going to take you home.' With that they jumped off the seat, held out their hands – I can see them now – and came with me without further ado. I felt very emotional about it all. I just wanted to pick them up and run away with them.

But Irene did not give in to her impulse. When everything was in order she and the girls crossed London and boarded a train for Wales. Although poorly dressed, the twins has arrived in London spotlessly clean, and what was more Irene understood that they had behaved themselves impeccably on the long journey. Unable to speak to her foster children, she consoled herself with the fact that she could at least offer them the refreshments she had prepared beforehand. A few hours later they were in Cardiff, the girls having

spent much of the time gazing out at the lush green countryside.

'When they arrived at our home,' the Reverend Mann
would later say, 'I was of course there to meet them. I fell
very much in love with them right away – for they were dear
children indeed.'

As Susi and Lotte were being prepared for bed that first
evening of their new life, it was quite obvious that they were
very weak, especially Susi. She had become so thin that the
Manns could count her ribs with ease. Lotte, who seemed
somewhat hardier, had rather more body fat and was one-
and-a-half inches taller. The Manns summoned their doctor,
who immediately explained that, as a result of malnutrition,
Susi and Lotte were in great danger of developing rickets.
He added that because both girls were deficient in calcium,
the bones in their legs were nowhere near as strong as they
should have been.

Before the twins' arrival the Manns had befriended a
Jewish couple, the Vellishes, themselves refugees from
Vienna. It was a relationship which was to prove invaluable,
because for the following three months Mrs Vellish would
turn up every single morning to speak in German with the
girls, outlining to them what Irene had planned for them
that day, as well as teaching them their first words of English.
The twins soon became very fond of her and, increasingly,
of their foster parents too.

That first summer Irene threw herself with great enthusiasm and energy into her new role as a mother.

In the afternoons I would take them out. I was obliged to get a
double pram, though, because it was just impossible to take
them for a normal walk – they simply didn't have the strength
in their legs. I put them side by side and said to myself:
'Right, I don't care what other people think – at least like this
they'll get some fresh air.' One and a half miles away we had a
park, where we would go and feed the ducks, and I would

point out the flowers and talk in English to them. It took me no time at all to love the children. But I felt that the important thing was not to force ourselves on them, but to win them over gradually. It all seemed to go well, for they were as happy as the day was long.

The new foster parents soon detected in the girls the same character traits that had been so evident at the Antonien-heim. Whereas Lotte was warm and outgoing, Susi was clearly more timid and withdrawn. 'The twins were so opposite,' Irene recalls. 'Nor were they really close. Once I could see in the garden that Lotte had her two arms around Susi. She was rocking her and, half in English, half in German, she was saying: "Susi, my Susi, meine Schwester, mein lovely sister..." and Susi was sitting there like a little statue, just enduring it, and clearly waiting for the ordeal to come to an end.'

During the twins' first autumn in Wales, war had been declared. All the while their English was improving, but the same could not be said of their health. Over the following months they both succumbed on four occasions to bronchitis, a weakness which the family's GP was quick to attribute to the change in climate between Munich and the Welsh capital.

'My wife made every provision for their health and strengthening, and I did my part too,' the Reverend Mann recalls. 'For one whole year, if not more, at 5.30 in the morning my wife rose and pressed out an orange, and took the juice into the children's bedroom, where they drank it readily and happily. This seemed to help quite considerably, for slowly they began to gain strength.'

Within twenty-four hours of settling into their new home, the twins had been kitted out with new sets of clothes. The heavy Germanic boots and thick white cotton underwear in which they had arrived were discreetly put aside. 'I felt that they must be made to look as English as possible in order to mix with other children,' their foster mother remembers. 'We bought them complete new outfits, but always dressed them alike.'

Some months before receiving the twins, the Manns had been asked to attend an interview in London with members of the children's refugee committee. During a lengthy discussion the committee expressed concern that the sisters would be baptized. Indeed was this not inevitable, they asked, with a prospective father who was a Baptist minister? The Reverend Mann soon found himself giving a hasty tutorial on the practices of the Baptist Church. Contrary to popular belief, he explained, it does not baptize infants into the Christian faith; nor has it ever sought to do so. Thus he was able to reassure the committee that there was no possibility whatsoever of Susi and Lotte being baptized in the name of Jesus Christ. With a collective sigh of relief, the committee declared itself reassured by the Reverend's words.

All non-Jewish prospective foster parents were required to give an undertaking not to convert their foster child. In fact they were asked to endeavour to maintain to the best of their ability his or her Jewish identity. Here again the Manns were able to satisfy the committee. However, whereas they were to remain true to their pledge not to baptize the girls, on the issue of their Jewish identity they were not to fare so well. For as soon as the twins set foot in their new home their Hebraic roots were quietly forgotten, never to be mentioned again. The Manns were in no doubt: Susi and Lotte were to grow up as Christians, attending Sunday school and participating fully in their church's many activities.

Before long the ancient Hebrew songs the girls had heard so often at the orphanage began to fade from their minds. They were replaced by the hymns and powerful singing of the Welsh chapel, where darkness, death and burning hell were never far from the lips of the fiery preacher who was now their father. The Reverend Mann had not the slightest desire to broadcast the fact that he and his wife had taken in German Jewish children. And he did not.

While Susi and Lotte were lucky to have escaped with their lives, much had already been lost to them, despite their tender age. Abandoned by their father before their birth, they had experienced precious little bonding with their natural mother. True, the Antonienheim had become familiar and given them a degree of security. But now that too was gone. And inevitably, as the months passed, their grasp of their native language began to falter. At the same time a subtle campaign of attrition was allowing their Jewish roots likewise to pass into oblivion. Was there anything left to be stripped from the twins?

Indeed there was, for their official identities were also in process of being transformed. It had all been planned. Although of course they would not have understood it, by the time they arrived in Cardiff their birth-names had been struck from the record – at least in the minds of their foster parents if not legally. In fact it was to take most of two decades to complete the process, although the clear intention took effect from the start. The Manns had no difficulty in convincing themselves that their reasoning was sound and in the best interests of the twins. The last thing they wanted, they were quick to agree, was for the girls to be persecuted or punished in some way for having names that were manifestly not British in origin. The very idea of putting them at risk in this way was unthinkable, and all the more so now that Britain and Germany were at war.

And yet instead of simply calling Lotte Lottie, and Susi Susan, the Manns decided on a more radical solution. The giving of completely new names served their purpose well, for it wiped the slate clean. A new, non-German, non-Jewish life was to be forged for the twins, one wholly untainted by the rather unsavoury middle-European past to which the couple had been made party. Thus it was that Lotte meta-morphosed into Eunice Mary, while Susi was henceforth to be known as Grace Elizabeth, a name to honour a Christian virtue.

Anxious to present an ideal image of happy family life to a sometimes inquisitive world, the Manns now found it imperative to bury all links with the girls' Bechhöfer ancestry. For anyone who might ask awkward questions, the Manns' answer was brief. Hardly anything was known: the orphanage in Munich had been destroyed by fire three weeks after the twins had arrived in Cardiff, and all the records with it.

However, the fantasy went further, for the Reverend would become extremely irritable if anyone suggested, directly or indirectly, that Eunice and Grace were anything but his own flesh and blood. And this despite the fact that it is not easy to explain the sudden arrival of two three-year-old children in a family. He would defend his claim to true paternity with such vigour that sometimes it seemed that he had succeeded in convincing himself. And if, from time to time, this spirited defence demanded a white lie or two to bolster the myth, then so be it. After all, was it not in the best interests of the girls?

And to Susi, the twin to whom the Reverend Mann now began to devote an increasing amount of time and affection, to the point of possessiveness, her foster father's message could not have been clearer. 'Remember one thing and you will not go wrong,' he would repeatedly instil in the more fragile of his charges. 'That your name is Grace Elizabeth Mann and you are mine.'

THREE

House Rules

In Cardiff tongues were beginning to wag. At least that was the message reaching the Reverend and Mrs Mann. In fact, unbeknown to them, the gossip had been going on for the best part of two years, ever since they had taken in the young refugees from Germany. Perhaps they had been naïve, for from the outset their ambition had been that their foster daughters should become indistinguishable from the other children in the vicinity, and that they should slip quietly into the Welsh way of life. In short, their fervent hope was that not one finger would be pointed at the twins, questioning their origins or singling them out from their peers. But such hopes would soon be dashed.

Little Eunice, now five years old, had been the first to let the cat out of the bag. As Irene Mann was towelling her after a bath, Eunice looked into her eyes with an intensity that made it clear she was seeking some kind of reassurance.

'Mummy,' she asked, 'what is German?'

It was exactly the kind of question Irene had hoped never to hear. Struggling to keep her composure, she decided to make light of it.

'Why do you ask?' she replied as casually as she could.

'Because there's a girl at school who keeps saying to us

that we're German. She says her father thinks because we're at war with Germany we should go back to our own country.'

When Edward Mann returned from chapel that evening he was furious. Eunice's innocent curiosity threatened to undermine everything he was trying to achieve for the twins. For him, fostering and adoption were akin to state secrets – not a matter for public debate. True, the taunting had come from just one five-year-old girl. But by her own admission she was repeating what was being said in her own home – and perhaps others. Ever decisive, the Reverend Mann was in no doubt about what had to be done: if his daughters were not to be permitted to mix easily with their school friends, then they must change school.

'Right,' he thundered. 'They're too near the house, and they're too near the church, where everybody knows who they are and what they are.'

Within a week Eunice and Grace had been dispatched to a smart private school some distance away. Arrangements were made to transport the twins to and from school each day. But the Manns were sure that such efforts, in addition to the unaccustomed burden of school fees, were worthwhile, and indeed very soon the girls were thriving in a new environment where no one need know about their background.

But a change of schools was no magic wand. Some two-and-a-half years later, questions arose that the Manns thought had been buried long ago. And this time the twins were united in their quest. They had spent some time talking together about what was bothering them, and one evening asked whether 'Mummy and Daddy are our real Mummy and Daddy'. But unlike Eunice's earlier question, which had caught Irene completely off guard, this one was to receive a more thoughtful reply. It would be in the form of a story, Irene promised the twins, which she would tell them as soon as they were in bed. That evening Eunice and Grace could hardly get into their nightclothes fast enough.

'Once upon a time,' their mother began, 'there was a very wicked man indeed, called Adolf Hitler. He was the leader of this country called Germany, and he was doing all sorts of cruel things to men, women and children alike. He just wanted power for himself and he was very cruel. So a lot of children were sent away from Germany so that they wouldn't get into his clutches – and you were amongst them. And that was how you came to us – it was all done properly, of course – so that you could have a happy upbringing.'

Eunice, warm and exuberant as always, needed no prompting. She immediately got out of bed and flung her arms around her mother. 'I'm so glad that God gave us you and Daddy,' she said joyfully. 'Isn't it wonderful!'

With such an enthusiastic response to her little story, Irene could have been excused for thinking that a very delicate problem had been dealt with once and for all, and for feeling relieved that there would be no more awkward questions about origins, identity and suchlike. So moved had she been by Eunice's display of affection that she had paid scant attention to Grace's quite different reaction to the story. Withdrawing into herself even more than usual, Grace had not uttered a single word – either of gratitude or reproach. But then, Irene told herself, such a mood was typical of Grace, always bottling up her feelings so.

By the spring of 1945 Germany had been roundly defeated and its cities lay in ruins. Hitler's monstrous reign was over. Together with the rest of war-weary Britain, the Reverend and Mrs Mann were looking forward to a prolonged period of peace and stability. Sadly, however, far from being able to bask in the sunshine of victory, the Manns were about to engage in a cruel struggle of their own – not on the battlefields of Europe but beside a hospital bed.

It all began innocently enough. When the twins had arrived, in 1938, Eunice had been slightly taller than Grace.

Over the years Grace had slowly but steadily closed the gap and in fact had now overtaken her sister. The Manns did not make much of it, knowing that children's growth rates are unpredictable. Nor did the twins. But then Grace noticed another change in her sister: she herself could easily run to catch the bus to school, whereas Eunice would often struggle to keep up. As time went by Eunice's movements seemed to become more and more uncoordinated, and she developed a marked limp. Nor was there much respite at night, when she would often have bouts of vomiting for no apparent reason.

Night after night the whole family's sleep was disturbed, but what concerned everyone most was the mystery of what was wrong with Eunice. The Manns had no idea what to do. 'Come on, Eunice,' one or other of them would say somewhat lamely, 'there really is no need for all of this.' They suspected that the many changes in her physical abilities and her behaviour, some of which seemed quite irrational, were probably psychological in origin. At the same time they were aware that if this was not the case, she could be suffering from some no less worrying physical disorder.

Eunice's behaviour had indeed become bizarre. No longer a small child, she had a compulsion to ask, quite unabashed, inappropriate questions of complete strangers. She considered it her business, for example, to know what someone was planning to eat that evening. This and other eccentricities made Grace feel her sister was slipping away from her – and the worst part was there was nothing she could do for her.

It was Eunice's headmistress who was the first to realize that her pupil was not a wilfully disruptive girl. 'That child needs a doctor, Mrs Mann,' she told her mother.

And so the Manns embarked on a circuit of medical consultations that would become all too familiar. First one general practitioner was visited, then another. Then one paediatrician, followed by a second. To add to the strain on the family, Grace was also required to attend each time, and asked to perform physical tests for the purpose of comparison and to determine whether she too was suffering from the same illness. Time after time doctors shook their heads ponderously and suggested yet another series of tests with another specialist. And still nobody could pinpoint the problem.

Eventually Eunice was seen by an eminent neurosurgeon, and that was when the family received the verdict they had been dreading. Scarcely nine years old, and the subject of one ghastly test after another without ever bemoaning her fate, Eunice displayed all the classic symptoms of a malignant brain tumour.

'It's difficult to describe exactly how we felt,' Irene would later recall, 'other than to say it shattered us completely. It was as if the bottom had dropped out of our world.'

Professor Lambert-Rogers, of Cardiff's Royal Infirmary, was quite clear: surgery was required as a matter of the utmost urgency. Drawing strength from their faith in the Almighty, the Manns accepted that they had no alternative but to agree: it was a matter of life or death. They signed the consent form.

When Eunice came round after several hours of surgery, her head shaved, she became hysterical. 'Mummy, Mummy,' she called out, sensing Irene's presence beside her bed. 'I'm blind. I can't see you! I can't see anything or anybody!'

It was true. The doctors were quick to explain that it was the shock to the brain. More specifically, reducing the pressure exerted by the tumour had caused the optic nerve to cease functioning. But, it was emphasized, she would regain her sight within twenty-four hours, and when Irene returned the next day Eunice was sitting up in bed smiling, cheery as always, and able to see again. Even so, Eunice was the first person to admit that she looked a dreadful sight, swathed in bandages and with an enormous, turban-like dressing on her head.

If the Manns had hoped that this single surgical intervention would conclude the matter, they were disappointed. Professor Lambert-Rogers informed them that a second operation was imperative, for all that had been done so far was to remove a piece of the cranium to let the tumour have its way. The next step was to attack the tumour itself.

This time, after a complicated four-hour operation, Eunice lay unconscious for three weeks. To reduce her temperature, she lay naked, with just a light cotton sheet above and below her fragile frame. All day and every day Irene sat at her bedside, keeping vigil, hoping and praying for her daughter either to open her eyes or, if it was God's will, to stop breathing for ever. Little Eunice must have decided that her life had not yet run its course, for after what seemed an infinity to her family she opened her eyes, looked up and smiled.

With Eunice still engaged in her struggle to survive, the Manns decided that it was important for Grace to be released from the suffocating atmosphere of illness, and their doctor readily agreed. They were convinced that she would be happier at a boarding school, well away, for the time being, from her sickly twin. It would be a healthier way of life for Grace, and it would enable Irene to devote her time and energy to the sister who needed it most.

Not for the first time in her life, Grace felt the pain of separation. Once again she was leaving the world that she knew, the people and places that gave shape to her life. Although greatly distressed as she said her goodbyes, even as her father was driving her to her new school she resolved to survive.

Shunted off to Somerset, that first night Grace lay in her bed in the stark and chilly dormitory of Yeovil's private Park School feeling bewildered and alone. Once again her world had been turned upside down. In time, however, she evolved

34

a strategy for coping: to make others smile, and to bring mischievous fun and laughter to every situation. It certainly won friends for her, and more than one of the teachers fell under her spell – even as they wrung their hands in despair over what should be done with her. At bottom it was all a way of securing attention, and it gave Grace a heady, alive feeling even when that attention brought punishment with it. And yet if she craved anything more than to be noticed it was to be loved.

During her first term Grace seldom passed an undisturbed night. The reluctant boarder had a number of worries on her mind, and they loomed especially large during the hours of darkness. One particular nightmare recurred endlessly. She dreamt that her sight had been wrested from her, just as Eunice had briefly lost hers. Surely it was only a matter of time, strange, recurring images would suggest, before she too was wheeled off to the operating theatre. Sweating profusely, she would emerge from her half-sleep urgently in need of someone to tell her it was only a dream. But in the enclosed world of the British boarding school, no such soothing voice was to be heard.

As the Reverend Mann's posts changed, so too did Grace's schools. From Yeovil she was moved to an institution noted for laying great emphasis on Christian ethics: Clarendon School, in North Wales.

The five years Grace was to spend at Clarendon turned out to be the most magical period of her childhood. Although entirely secluded, the school's setting was majestic, with the rolling Welsh countryside all around and the sea within sight. The entrance to the school's grounds opened on to a large expanse of open park land. When delivering their daughters, parents would turn into this concealed entrance, off a long and winding lane, and the approach of a car was always an exciting event, betrayed by the sound of its wheels negotiating a sheep grid set in the road. If the girls missed that clue, they could hardly fail to notice the sound of a car coming to a halt on the gravel outside the main door. On entering the main building in winter, the visitor would be greeted by a log fire glowing beneath the finely crafted wood panelling.

Clarendon's regime was strict. The girls' reading material was drawn from the Christian and Classical traditions, with little input from the outside world. Prayers were said regularly, and every girl was expected to attend. For the older pupils there were additional laws, rigorously enforced, outlawing dancing and the wearing of make-up. And yet, despite the austerity and repression of the girls' natural femininity, for the first time in her life Grace felt both happy and free. Much to her parents' regret, though, her studies were a matter of supreme indifference to her. She was too busy enjoying herself, for she had overcome her earlier sense of exile and isolation and was now rejoicing in the feeling of freedom.

Manners, as Grace was known to friend and foe alike, soon established herself as a personality. Now coming up to eleven years of age, she was emerging from her shell with a vengeance, driven partly by the need to make up for lost time. Always misbehaving and in trouble with the teachers, she rapidly developed a reputation for her quick wit and repartee. Such skills might not have been what her parents had envisaged, yet there was no denying that in terms of strength of character and self-esteem Grace was making remarkable progress.

However, in a dramatic reversal of mood she would become very downcast as the end of each term drew near, and with it the prospect of going home for a few weeks. Grace had come to dread the atmosphere of the Manns' household, and in particular the daily threat of falling foul of one of her father's thunderous rages. For the Reverend Mann the opposite was true: he always looked forward keenly to the day of his daughter's return. And always, once she was home, he would immediately set about reiterating certain fundamental rules – just in case they had faded from her mind while she had been away. It was a crucial message that she had heard many times before.

'Remember, Grace, that you are never to mention the word "adoption". There's no need to. It's a big, big secret that you must never tell anybody. You won't, will you? Promise me now. Because you are mine, and I want everybody to believe that you are mine.'

Having received the pledge that he desperately needed to hear – all the more so since both girls had once asked him whether he and his wife were their real parents – the Reverend was satisfied for a while. His secret, it seemed, was safe.

Edward Mann was rather clever with words. Many a student at Wightside, the evangelical Bible college on the edge of Manchester where he was now Principal, would have testified to that. What the Reverend Mann said, he meant. Therefore Grace could not fail to be aware that she was his personal property. And not only did Irene appear to accept her husband's proprietorial claim: she actively colluded in reinforcing it. For example, she would emphasize to anyone visiting the house that any invitation to Grace that would take her away from her home, however briefly, would first have to be vetted by her husband. The Reverend seldom deigned to grant her an exit visa. On the contrary, he enforced a regime so restrictive and severe that it began to make Clarendon, for all its tightly drawn rules and regulations, seem like a holiday camp.

At home during the school holidays, Grace found herself a prisoner in her father's study, for it was there she had to remain so as to be at his beck and call. Strictly forbidden to form friendships with children of her own age, indeed deprived of the chance to develop outside relationships of

any kind, she was even discouraged from reading newspapers
and magazines. And within that study, bursting with theological and Scriptural texts, Grace would have another of the
Reverend Mann's cardinal rules drummed into her time after
time: 'Don't talk to anybody else, Grace.' The common
purpose of all these prohibitions was simple: he wanted
Grace entirely for himself. Lines of demarcation had been
drawn up in the Mann household: while Irene tended to the
needs of Eunice, Edward was responsible for Grace's welfare.
This duty he took seriously, and it is clear that many of his
impulses towards her displayed genuine care and dedication.

But, as the years went by, the Reverend became more and
more besotted, and eventually obsessed, with Grace. And
since this was an arrangement which served his purposes
very well, it became unthinkable to him even to contemplate
setting her free. A complex man, proud and very emotional,
he would repeatedly declare his love for his foster daughter.
It was, however, a love that placed a heavy burden on the
young girl. 'You mean so much to me,' he would tell her. 'I
do love you so much. I don't ever want you to leave me. You
won't ever leave me, will you, Grace?'

Part of Grace recoiled from such possessiveness. Suffocated by her father's demands, she always counted the days
until her return to Clarendon. And yet another part of her
responded more readily to his apparent devotion. Desperate
for love and approval, and as a result constantly fearful of
rejection, she realized that his repeated declarations had
begun to touch her. She had found someone who cared. The
fact is, Grace had learned to compartmentalize her life, being
outgoing, sometimes provocatively so, at school, and yet
regressing into submission to her father's will at home.

Yet the relationship was by no means all darkness and
torment for Grace: there were positive aspects too. On occasion the Reverend would not hesitate to back his daughter in
the event of a showdown between her and Irene; and every

now and then he would hand her a half-crown to spend on herself. In addition, despite the severity of her father's regime and all it demanded of her, somehow she felt she was able to communicate rather well with him.

Fearful as she was of crossing her father, Grace nevertheless felt proud of him when he stood in the pulpit preaching to his congregation. His sermons were full of kindness and Christian compassion of a high order. But this message was not restricted to words, for he was a man of action too. Towards the end of the 1930s, in the period immediately after the twins had arrived safely from Germany, the Reverend had felt moved to carry out further work with refugees. He and Irene had helped to secure the release and resettlement in England and Wales of no fewer than ten other refugees from what he always referred to as 'Hitler's hell'. Six of these were children, two were doctors and one an architect of great distinction. The Manns' determined fight to uphold fundamental human rights put to shame many Jewish families living in Britain at that time.

For all this, for Grace a return to Clarendon was a return to tranquillity. The prisoner of her father's study was now free once more. Friendships, forbidden at home, could be enjoyed again. Grace was close to many girls of her own age and together they had a wonderful time, although Grace's rebelliousness often lead them all into trouble. Some of them knew of Eunice's existence and felt very sorry for their friend, realizing how difficult it must have been to have a twin who was desperately ill and yet out of reach most of the time. But not even Grace's closest confidante knew anything of her dark and hidden past. Keeping her promise to her father, she revealed nothing.

By contrast, the school authorities knew all about her. As they were well aware, the law dictated that foreign children could not be formally adopted until they had reached the age of eighteen. Thus the one word guaranteed to send the

Reverend into a fit of anger – 'adoption' – should not have troubled him at all. If anything, it was fostering that should have been the unmentionable, for the twins had only ever been foster children. What was more, the names Grace Elizabeth and Eunice Mary had been given to them informally by the Manns and had no legal status whatsoever. The same was true of the girls' surname. On all relevant official documents, therefore, the names Susi and Lotte Bechhöfer lived on, as Grace was about to discover. This was the one remaining part of the twins' heritage that he had been unable to obliterate, much to his regret. Even the charismatic and influential preacher was powerless before the law.

It was the summer of 1954, and sixteen-year-old Grace entered the school hall to sit her GCE O-level examination in English Literature. She was apprehensive, like the dozens of other girls facing the same ordeal. Told to line up in alphabetical order, Grace took her place among the M's, but was immediately called to one side.

'Grace, today you're going to be with the B's,' said Miss Weston, a teacher Grace knew well, in a matter-of-fact tone.

Grace was puzzled. 'Why?' she asked.

'Susi Bechhöfer – well, that's your real name,' Miss Weston explained, pointing to the unfamiliar name on the piece of paper in her hand.

As she clutched the paper the teacher had given her, Grace's mind raced back to the time when, eight years earlier, her mother had explained why Grace and Eunice had left Germany and settled with her and their father. Then she remembered that nothing more had been said since then. The girls had asked no further questions, and no other information had been volunteered by the Manns.

As she filed slowly along the corridor leading to the examination room, now rubbing shoulders with Baker and Brown, Grace felt stunned and humiliated – and all the more because she was among her friends. Most people liked

Manners very much indeed. But how on earth would she be able to explain her situation to her classmates? Surely her popularity could only suffer. And yet to launch into an explanation was unthinkable, for how many times had she been told that it was strictly forbidden to say anything at all about her past?

Every year, come examination time, the same words would crop up, as if for their annual airing. Perhaps it was a co-incidence that most of the teachers at Clarendon used the same phrase: good passes in the GCEs were, they stressed, the girls' 'passports to the future'. Despite this pressure, for the ninety minutes of the English Literature exam Grace sat in a daze, staring out of the window, unable to write a single word except for the strange-sounding name she had copied from Miss Weston's piece of paper. She looked at it again and again: 'Susi Bechhöfer'. Had she not seen those two words somewhere before, tucked away in a drawer at home, on a ration book from the war years? And had she not seen those two funny dots over the 'o' once or twice? She was not sure. Yet they struck some dim and distant chord in her memory. At the same time the name Mann was buzzing around in her head. That was her name; it would just not do to dispense with it like that. It was as if Edward Mann was sitting beside Grace in the examination hall, for he could not have put it more succinctly himself.

As the minutes ticked by, her pen refusing to budge, Grace felt that she was completely different from the other girls, as if her clandestine, almost criminal past had finally caught up with her. Unlike all the others, she apparently possessed a dual identity. The skeleton in the cupboard, which her father had tried so hard to keep from her, had insisted on making an appearance after all. Not only was this sudden turn of events very distressing for Grace; it could not have come at a worse moment. Here was one girl who would not be receiving her passport to the future.

For the rest of the exam Grace dwelled on her past. One thing she was sure of: the identity of Susi Bechhöfer did not appeal to her in the least. In any case, everything was so much more straightforward as Grace Mann. Whoever she was and wherever she came from, Susi Bechhöfer surely had nothing to contribute. There was no room in Grace's life for this interloper whose sudden presence augured only trouble. The fact was that the very sound of the name sent painful memories flashing through Grace's mind – memories of being described by her school friends as looking 'foreign'; memories of learning as a child that she had been brought to Britain from a far-away place called Munich, in a frightening country called Germany. All in all, the sooner Susi was cast aside, the better. The Reverend Mann's great secret might have been laid bare, but for the present it had emerged unscathed. And it was Grace's refusal to acknowledge Susi's existence that he could thank for that.

Grace's past was not the only secret father and daughter shared. In other areas too the Reverend had sworn her to secrecy. He had good reason to demand her silence. As he knew full well, if the truth were to be discovered he would not only be stripped of his clerical collar, but would find himself behind bars. For ever since the diagnosis of Eunice's illness, the head of the Bible College had been had been unable or unwilling to restrain himself from seeing Grace in a different light. No longer just someone to whom he was closely attached, she had become for the Reverend a sexual being, and therefore a potential means of gratifying his own desires. Here was the real reason why he was so determined that Grace should not stray from his study when she was at home. For in that closed room she could be trained to tend to his needs. Nor would she dare refuse him.

Grace, remembering the rapport they had until recently enjoyed, tried to continue to be a normal daughter to him, but the Reverend had changed the rules. Constantly demanding more, he wanted her to play the role of his lover as well as his child.

'Grace, I can come into your bed tonight, can't I?' he would ask as a matter of course. It did not occur to Grace that this was a request which she might have been able to refuse. Nor indeed that she might appeal to someone for help. Not only was she completely terrified of her father – a look from him could send her scuttling up the stairs – but she was also barely nine years old when he first made such demands. Once in her bed, he cast aside all pretence of self-control.

Just as the Reverend's black moods would spring up from nowhere, so too would his sexual desire. Nor was the abuse confined to the night. In fact, it occurred more often during the daytime, in his study, although that was by no means the only place. In the early days Grace dutifully obeyed him, although she came to loathe him for it. But as she entered her teens, she did at least pluck up the courage to ask why she should have to perform such tasks. The Reverend's reasoning, grotesque and distorted though it was, served to convince her to carry on, for that was what mattered to him.

'Because if you do this to me, Grace,' he would explain, 'it makes me feel that you are my own child. You know that the greatest tragedy of my life has been that I haven't been able to have children of my own. So if you do this for me, it just makes me feel that much closer to you.'

The Reverend had developed a habit which he practised with great skill. Should any opportunity present itself for sexual contact with his daughter, he found himself both unable and unwilling to resist it, even if the setting was well removed from the relative security of his study. Perhaps a public setting made the abuse even more exciting. Or perhaps it served to illustrate all the more vividly to Grace how he was able to control and manipulate her at his whim.

How else to explain a Baptist minister abusing his daughter in the shabby surroundings of the public swimming baths at Penarth, near Cardiff?

No wonder the Reverend looked forward to Grace's return during the school holidays; nor that she contemplated them with a heavy heart. Once she was back, he would lose little time in resuming his advances. On one occasion, having met Grace from her train, he drove straight to a nearby chemist's shop, mindful that contraception was in order now that Grace was reaching puberty.

No wonder, too, that the Reverend could never find anything positive to say about any teenage boy who expressed an interest in his daughter. Seldom did his refrain vary, no matter how impeccable the suitor's character and credentials.

'No, Grace, definitely not for you. Definitely not for you,' he would insist.

The reason for these repeated refusals was not difficult to detect. Even the idea of his daughter being wooed by another man made the minister of religion desperately jealous. He wanted her all to himself. Had he not made his terms clear many years earlier?

In order to buy Grace's loyalty, the Reverend relied on the powerful weapon of the implied threat: 'Because if you don't do as I say, Grace...' Of course he never went on to spell out what might befall her should she refuse. For Grace, the worst thing was not knowing what sanctions might follow. Ignorant of what reprisals might be in store, she was at the mercy of her fertile imagination, as the Reverend had intended. Was it not possible, the agonizing thought occurred to her, that Grace Mann, like Susi Bechhöfer before her, would be cast aside, consigned to the past?

The Reverend's strategy was to serve him very well, because for more than a decade Grace did not utter a word about her predicament to anyone. Throughout these years it remained a secret.

Towards the end of her teens, however, Grace began to feel differently about what had happened to her, and much of the anger repressed since childhood began to surface. And yet Grace was unable to summon the courage to confront her father about the pain he was causing her. For the Reverend continued to exercise a powerful, almost hypnotic control over her every move. For all that she was a young woman now, rather than a child, she was still struggling in vain to break free.

Her feeling of revulsion reached a peak when one day when the Reverend Mann spoke to Eunice in a tone that Grace felt to be full of bitter accusation.

'Eunice,' he bellowed, unable to control the fury welling inside him. 'You have got cancer.'

Crying to herself, Eunice limped up the stairs. 'I haven't,' was all she could say.

As the Reverend raged – all the while seeming to Grace more and more like an animal – Irene busied herself in the kitchen. It was an all too familiar scene. Having delivered his blow, he would withdraw, stricken with remorse, awash with guilt and grief at the brutal savagery of his tongue. The furious moods that would descend on the minister seemed to come from nowhere – and the result was always the same: a black cloud would hover over the whole household, although Irene would carry on as if nothing had happened.

Appalled by her father's unfeeling treatment of her ailing sister, Grace could stand no more. Without a word she walked into his study, picked up the telephone and began to dial 999 – to talk to the police. Now the truth concerning her father's sexual abuse would be revealed. But as she did so the minister walked into the room. Lost in his own troubled thoughts, he did not see Grace, who silently replaced the receiver and crept out of the room, feeling at the same time relieved and thwarted.

Afterwards Grace dwelt for a long time on what had

45

happened. She realized as she made for the phone that should she report her father's behaviour and a criminal prosecution ensue, she would be responsible for triggering two important consequences. First, there would be an enormous scandal within the ranks of the Baptist Church. Now, as she thought about it afterwards, this outcome scarcely troubled her.

By contrast, the second prospect did. With the Reverend Mann almost certain to be detained at Her Majesty's pleasure, there would be no one to provide for Eunice. And that was one extra burden Grace was not prepared to add to her already heavy load. It was out of loyalty to her sister, she realized, rather than concern for her father, that she had replaced the receiver.

For the Reverend Mann it had been a narrow escape: once again he had been saved from public exposure.

FOUR

Obsessed

Throughout the twins' late childhood and teens Eunice continued to be very ill. Much of the time she was in great pain, and Irene would administer the most powerful medication available, in an attempt to relieve her suffering. Eunice often called out in the middle of the night: 'Mummy, Mummy, I don't know where I am.' Instantly she received the reassurance she sought. But by the time Irene had returned to her bed, Eunice was anxiously shouting for her again, completely disorientated, her mother's words of comfort having already faded from her mind. The days too were seldom without trauma, mainly because for several years Eunice suffered almost continuously from seizures which would cause her to drop to the floor, clutching her head and writhing in pain.

Nor, in this instance, had medical science been able to work its wonders. In fact, Eunice had hardly regained consciousness from her second operation when her parents were summoned to the consultant surgeon's room – a route they had come to know well. There they learned that the operation had not been carried out to his complete satisfaction – indeed he was not sure if it ever could be – but he felt it was his duty to try one more time.

Each time Eunice went into the operating theatre, her faithful Aunt Flora, who had kitted out the twins with clothes on their arrival in Wales, swung into action once more. Aware that Eunice felt very self-conscious shorn of her hair, Flora set about producing a series of little bonnets, including a yellow and pink pixie hat, of the same material and colouring as her clothes, so as to form a matching outfit. Flora's sewing skills were put to good and frequent use, for altogether Eunice was to have her hair removed seven times. And all to no avail.

'I'll never forget the day,' Irene would recall, 'after ten days in the Royal Infirmary, when the doctors produced the word "incurable". We drove off, with tears rolling down our faces, all the way home. Incurable – at just ten years of age.'

Having tried and failed, the surgeons admitted there was nothing more they could do. The patient could now return home; she would not have to face surgery again. Worst of all, the upshot of this string of interventions was that Eunice was extensively paralysed – not just in her legs, but also down her entire right side, so that she had only one good limb out of four. As a result, she would be wheelchair-bound for the rest of her life. The Manns, drawing strength from their Christian convictions, chose to take a positive view. At least now their daughter was no longer in pain. And although her body had all but ceased to operate, her mind remained intact – not least her cheerful disposition. For Eunice soon demonstrated that she did not intend to waste time bemoaning her fate. Quite the contrary: she attended a special Girl Guides group at a local hospital and even went to camps. In the process she grew to be dearly loved by those who came into contact with her. And she returned that love, as she did to her foster parents. Full of gratitude, she would often fling her good arm about her mother's neck and hug her tightly.

'Just forget it, my love,' Irene would reply, struggling to control her own emotions. 'We're glad to be able to do it for you. We just wish we could give you a new arm or a new leg.'

And then she would add a few extra words, because she knew they always comforted her daughter and brought a smile to her face. 'Never mind, my love: there'll be no wheel-chairs or wonky arms or legs in heaven.'

As devoted as Irene was to Eunice, so was she derelict in her duty towards Grace. Although she developed an uncanny knack of absenting herself on the occasions when her husband seemed likely to seek sexual favours from Grace, her intuition was far from fail-proof. On several occasions she walked in on father and daughter at a most inappropriate moment, with the result that all three parties were covered in confusion and embarrassment. Almost every time, as Grace quietly slipped away, a fierce argument would erupt between the Reverend and his wife, their angry words reverberating around the household.

Afterwards Grace would receive not a word of sympathy or support from her mother. On the contrary, like her father before her, she soon found herself at the mercy of Irene Mann's sharp tongue. Underlying these attacks was Irene's painful realization that her foster daughter had become a rival for her husband's affections, and a formidable one at that. In her mother's eyes, therefore, there was little that Grace could do, try as she might, to win even her most meagre approval.

Irene Mann might have failed in terms of mothering Grace, but she also had a raw deal as a wife. Not only had her husband forsaken her bed; she also had the humiliation of knowing precisely where and with whom he was likely to be at night. In fact, during the school holidays the Reverend had a habit of abandoning the marital bed altogether in favour of a spare room a little way along the corridor of their flat, so as to be opposite Grace's bedroom.

It was hardly surprising that Grace found it difficult to forge anything like a normal relationship with her foster mother. Likewise, while Irene displayed genuine love and tenderness towards Eunice, she could rarely find it in herself to show affection to her other daughter. In any case her husband would not have permitted it, for his practice of excluding all rivals for Grace's affection had not altered with the passage of time. Grace was not to be shared – not even with her mother. 'Sometimes you would think that those two were lovers,' said Mavis Wainman, a visitor to the family home – an observation which must have hurt Grace's mother, innocent though it was.

The destructive undercurrents flowing through the Mann household eventually began to take their toll on Irene. Tending to Eunice day and night was extremely draining in itself. But in addition to that duty the Reverend's wife was obliged to be available to counsel female students at the Bible College, many of whom wished to consult her about their own personal problems. It was a role which she carried out with much skill and aplomb. But with no one to counsel her in her own difficulties, and unwilling to reveal the dark secrets of her own marriage, Irene began to show more and more signs of stress, experiencing bouts of hyperventilation and falling to the floor in hysterical paralysis. It was not long before she herself was confined to bed, diagnosed as suffering from nervous exhaustion.

Mother and daughter, estranged from one another as they were, had one thing in common: neither had anyone at all with whom they could share their sense of isolation – least of all each other.

At the same time, despite Grace's concern for Eunice, all was not sweetness and light between the twins. For many years there had been considerable tension, for although she rarely said as much, Grace resented the fact that her sister had become both disfigured and incapacitated. Previously they had talked, walked and run together, whereas after the tumour was diagnosed these activities had ceased abruptly. As young children they had played happily together, with Eunice invariably the leader of the two, often protecting her more fragile sister in minor skirmishes at school. But those days had long since gone. The sad truth was that from the moment she had set eyes on her sister neatly propped up on pillows in her hospital bed after her first craniotomy, Grace had felt that her twin had already passed from her.

Eunice's illness had prompted Grace to make a painful reappraisal of their relationship. The situation had not been at all easy to accept, and when Grace was back at home from boarding school she would occasionally take out her frustration on her sister. There were frequent arguments, often concerning the family piano, a dark upright model to which she was very attached. Grace loved to play it, but Eunice could not bear what to her ears was a string of ugly, discordant sounds.

With Grace out of the way at school, Eunice naturally came increasingly under the influence of her mother, on whom she had become entirely dependent. As a result, during the school holidays it would not be long before Eunice was herself pointing her finger at her twin sister. 'That's a very unchristian thing to do,' she would often remark. And then, just to remind Grace of the many binding rules of the Mann household, she would warn her twin: 'Mummy and Daddy wouldn't like that.' For Grace, it seemed that her best and oldest friend had ceased to exist. Once again she had been abandoned.

For years Grace had been leading a double life, as is the fate of many a child sent away to boarding school. But for Grace, the contrast was unusually extreme. At Clarendon she enjoyed close and enduring friendships, laughter and fun. Awaiting her at home were an abusing and controlling father,

an invalid sister and a remote mother. However, when she
was fifteen and a half she was forced back into this nightmare full time, for the Manns had decided that she should
leave school. Based at home, she would attend the local technical college and sit the O-levels in English and French that
she had failed at Clarendon.

Grace's return home ushered in a period of despondency.
Not only did she find her studies dreary; what seemed to her
even worse, she felt a victim of her parents' shortage of
money. At a time when, like any teenager, she wanted to dress
up and enjoy herself, the Reverend made it abundantly clear
that she would have to make do with her school uniform,
comprising a shapeless dress, a V-necked sweater, striped
socks and distinctly unflattering shoes. Again and again she
was reminded that she was lucky to have as much as she did,
given the strain that Eunice's condition placed on the family
purse. In time Grace acknowledged the dilemma, and realized
that there was no point in complaining.

Throughout this period she struggled to maintain the
optimism she had known at Clarendon. But whereas at school
she had been buoyed up by constant companionship, now
she retreated into daydreams to lift her spirits. Sitting alone
in church, she would imagine a life in which she was free of
the sexual obligations imposed on her by a domineering
father, free of his rages, free of the petty restrictions in which
he sought to ensnare her.

For the Reverend Mann was as determined as ever to
have his daughter all to himself. In recent years he had
braced himself for the day when he would have to allow
Grace out into the world. How, he had often wondered,
would he be able to isolate and control her when her
school-days were over? Although it entailed a degree of
exposure to the wider world, the technical college was a
necessary step if Grace was to make something of herself.
At least, he could comfort himself, the clothes she wore to

class were hardly calculated to attract the attention of the opposite sex.

However, as soon as Grace's year at the college was over, the Reverend's possessiveness raised its head once more. After some thought he decided that the answer lay in the Girl Crusaders Union. Here was a Christian organization from which the male of the species was wholly barred; where only women, of varying ages, were to be found working diligently side by side. The Reverend used his influence to ensure that his daughter was appointed a junior office clerk, with a number of minor duties to perform. It was an ideal solution, he felt. But what about when the working day ended?

Ironically, it was indeed after office hours that Grace, now eighteen, fell in love for the first time. She had been aware for some time that young men had begun to notice her, but she had always turned her head away, remembering the lessons her father had drummed into her for so many years. Inside, though, she was quietly rebelling, planning her escape when the right person came along. He might not have been able to point to the most exciting of careers, but David Bond, a bank clerk from Thornton Heath, south London, and an active member of the Reverend Mann's own congregation, was such a young man, stirring feelings in Grace that she had never felt before.

Grace knew that any attempt to develop a friendship with David would meet with her father's strenuous opposition. Nevertheless, desperately keen to have the freedoms enjoyed by other girls of her age, she calculated that if she granted her father more sexual favours he might relax his veto. Eventually she was allowed to go on a date with David, but the plan backfired, for after giving his consent the Reverend became even more obsessed with his daughter and redoubled his efforts to thwart the relationship.

'He's just not the sort of person I want you to be involved with, Grace,' he said, plainly in no mood to argue. 'You can do far better than that,' he added, secretly hoping that he would not have to vet an alternative.

But her father's insistence was to no avail, because for the first time in her life Grace began to dare to defy his orders, by arranging a number of clandestine meetings with her new and ardent admirer. Tracking her every move, the Reverend did not take long to find out, and made no effort to conceal his wrath. Yet, sensing his daughter's determination, he indicated his willingness to adopt a different attitude. She could go out with her young man, but on certain conditions. So restrictive were these that the Reverend felt confident that the relationship would soon wither on the vine. Most importantly, Grace had to be home by 9.30 p.m., with the result that the young couple were scarcely able to enjoy an evening together.

In truth, the minister was as fascinated by this blossoming romance as he was horrified by it. He soon found himself unable to resist asking exactly how far the liaison had progressed. 'Has he kissed you yet?' he asked over dinner one evening, doing his best to make it sound like a casual enquiry. For if there had been any kissing, what other tokens of affection might the couple have exchanged? And what potentially damaging information might his daughter have confided to the young man? It was desperately important to find out. On this occasion the Reverend found out nothing incriminating at all – not even if Grace had received an innocent peck on the cheek – for Irene at once upbraided him for asking, thereby sparing her daughter the embarrassment of having to answer and frustrating her husband still further.

Bent on discomforting Grace's suitor in any way he could, one day the Reverend, on seeing the couple walking arm in arm in the street, went as far as to shout out: 'Young man, your arm!'

What else could he do to thwart their amour? the Reverend

wondered. Perhaps to impose one petty restriction after another was the answer, he decided.

'No, Grace, you certainly can't wear a string of pearls,' he summarily announced after inspecting his daughter's first romantic gift. 'I'll send them back.'

'No, Grace, he certainly cannot pay for you to subscribe to the tennis club. That is my job. I'll send the application back.'

The minister was convinced that a succession of such discouragements would eventually wear down the hapless bank clerk. However, soon after she had returned the artificial-pearl necklace and the tennis-club membership form, Grace learned that she was to enjoy a reprieve. For the Reverend, a highly respected figure in the world of Baptist nonconformism, had been invited to give a lecture-tour of the United States. Greatly flattered by the honour, he accepted – to his daughter's delight.

The organizers of the Reverend Mann's itinerary had pre-pared a punishing schedule involving nine flights and fifteen preaching engagements, all to be completed within twenty working days. In New York, then Buffalo, Chicago, Minneapolis and Los Angeles, the minister was deeply impressed by the vastness of the congregations before him. It was a far cry from preaching in the suburbs of Cardiff. In addition, their appreciation of his ministry was more warm and effusive than anything he had ever experienced in Britain. Likewise he encountered a far more open response in person-to-person contact with those who flocked to hear him.

The Reverend had cultivated a style of preaching which went down particularly well in the United States. Delivered in his deep and creamy Welsh tones, it was characterized by his customary force and conviction. Hand waving and pounding of the lectern helped to drive home to his audience his powerful message of compassion. Before long he was espousing a crucial tenet of American evangelism: that effective preaching is inextricably linked with effective finance. In this respect, thanks to the generosity of his various congregations, his tour was proving to be more fruitful than anything he had ever experienced in his church career. Indeed on one occasion, preaching at Wheaton, Illinois, on a Sunday morning, and then later at the evening service – both times with well over a thousand people present – he was handed a cheque for a sum so large that at first he was minded to refuse it altogether.

'But this is too much, surely,' he protested, only to be told that such sizeable offerings were standard practice in Wheaton, a city long recognized as a centre of religious activity and sometimes referred to as the 'Protestant Vatican of the Midwest'.

Did those three tumultuous weeks mean that Grace's relationship with David was able to proceed uninterrupted for a while at least? Not at all. For although the Reverend was thousands of miles away, he had no intention of giving up. He never gave up. It was just as just as well for him, therefore, that he still had one trump card up his sleeve.

He might have been on a whirlwind tour of America, struggling with a hectic schedule, but the Reverend still found time to write a series of letters to Grace. In these he reverted to his original tactic, repeatedly renewing his plea to his daughter to end her relationship with David. Steadfastly she refused. The letters were put aside and ignored. Finally, it seemed, Grace was breaking free.

One day soon after her father's return from his preaching tour, Grace arrived home from the Girl Crusaders Union to find her mother looking extremely pale and shaken. Had something happened to Eunice, she wondered. It had seemed likely for some time now.

'Daddy is very ill,' Irene explained, her tone indicating the gravity of the situation. Here was the Reverend's final card. And as it turned out, he had played it rather shrewdly. Daddy's illness was, in fact, self-inflicted. The Reverend had attempted suicide – still an indictable offence in the 1950s – by taking an overdose of drugs. Having failed, he was admitted to a clinic in Sussex, where he was diagnosed as suffering from a nervous breakdown. He had returned from America exhausted.

When Grace walked into her father's room at the clinic on a hot summer's day, wearing a favourite turquoise dress, she saw a man who looked vacant and unexpressive, utterly stripped of his usual charisma and air of authority. Somehow he managed to summon up the energy to utter a few words. Manipulative to the end, he grasped Grace's hand and whispered a plea she had heard many times before.

'You won't leave me, will you?'

'Of course not, Daddy,' she replied without hesitation.

Here, at last, were the words the Reverend had been waiting to hear. They proved to be far more healing than the electroconvulsive therapy that the clinic was beginning to administer to the preacher. Not so ill that he could not decipher a coded message, he knew that Grace was telling him, in her own way, that she was prepared to end the relationship that had caused him so much pain. For her part, Grace had decided that this was the least she could do, for was it not pitiful to see her father suffering so?

Edward Mann had got his own way once again. But the stakes had been high: it had been essential for his very survival to see that young man off. And now, at last, his sabotage had worked. Within six weeks of Grace's visit he had discharged himself from the clinic. The medical staff expressed dismay at his departure, which they considered premature, for he had not completed the course of treatment prescribed for him. They had no way of knowing that he had already received his cure.

This dramatic turn of events convinced David of what he

had long suspected: his pursuit of Grace was futile. Always strange towards him, the Reverend's behaviour had now made it impossible for David to have a normal relationship with his daughter. For her part, Grace, wrenched away from her first love, knew that the time had come to leave home. She had made up her mind to embark on a career in nursing, and enrolled on a three-year training course at the Oldchurch Hospital in Romford, Essex. The decision astounded her parents, who were not slow to point out that there had been little evidence of Grace's caring instincts in her dealings with Eunice. Surely, they argued, if she was genuinely interested in nursing, then who better to care for than her twin sister. In any case, Irene pleaded, she needed Grace to help her care for her sister. It was true that Eunice, still clinging doggedly to life, remained in desperate need of full-time care. Yet, anguished as she was by Eunice's plight, Grace felt that if she did not leave home and start to live her own life she would die too – in mind if not in body. It felt like a life for a life.

Clearly the Manns had failed to grasp Grace's real motivation, and she was not about to spell it out for them. What she wanted above all else was to get away from their suffocating grip, particularly that of her father. She had thought that a nursing career would provide a legitimate reason for going, but as far as she was concerned it could just as easily have been another kind of work altogether. In the event she stood her ground and stuck to her first choice.

The Manns may have capitulated, but throughout Grace's training, far from giving her encouragement, Irene would often play on her guilt about Eunice. How wonderful it would be, she said time and time again, if only Grace would give to her poor sister the care she lavished on her patients at the hospital.

Nor did Grace's escape from the Mann household effect the end of her father's obsession with her; indeed her absence seemed to exacerbate it. Although she gave up nearly every rest day to be with her parents, still the Reverend would ask when she was coming again, extracting a pledge from her to that effect. Grace could see that she was locked into a familiar pattern: as ever, it seemed to be her destiny to sacrifice herself to her father's emotional demands. And even worse than knowing how she would be spending every day off for the foreseeable future was being asked repeatedly to reassure her father that no, of course she would never leave him.

It was while in Birmingham, where she had gone to complete her midwifery training, that Grace became involved with Peter Bailey, a curate and, like David Pitts before him, also a member of her father's congregation. For the Reverend Mann, who by now had transferred his allegiance from the Baptist Church to the Church of England, a familiar threat loomed, except that with Grace now courting a clergyman the danger was even more pronounced. What if Bailey came to learn of the long years of abuse? Worse still, what if the Bishop were to hear of his misdemeanours? To begin with, the Reverend tried an approach that his daughter knew all too well.

'No, Grace, definitely not for you. You know that he's just been rejected by another girl and you would undoubtedly be on the rebound. I would hate to see you get hurt in that way.'

When that tack proved unsuccessful, and with Grace and Peter edging towards marriage – at least in the Reverend's imagination – Edward Mann embarked on another of his urgent, self-appointed missions of destruction. Fully recovered from his breakdown, he busied himself writing letters to Grace at the nurses' home and telephoning her incessantly. He then developed a habit of appearing on her doorstep without warning in order to plead with her in person. And on several occasions he suddenly emerged from the Birmingham traffic in his battered old Austin to spy on his daughter as she, on her bicycle, attempted to go about her business around the city.

For the Reverend it was imperative to bring his daughter's present relationship, like every one of them, to a speedy end. But in this case there was an even greater urgency than usual. As a man of the cloth, Peter Bailey could ruin the Reverend at a stroke if his dark secret were to come to light. The best form of defence seemed to be attack, the minister decided, and he wrote to the Bishop listing the reasons why his prospective son-in-law was quite unsuitable to become a vicar.

Here was a man possessed. No longer was he hounding a vulnerable, teenage schoolgirl, but a young woman of twenty-five – and evidently with some success, because it now appeared that he had managed to recruit his wife to his cause. For now she it was who sought to lay down the law to Grace.

'You do realize, don't you,' she told her daughter at the vicarage, 'that if you do go ahead and marry Peter, your father won't come to the wedding.' Grace stood stunned as Irene, somewhat superfluously, played her next card: the relationship was merely a friendship and any idea of marriage was really all in their heads. For instead of accepting the prospect of her father's absence from the ceremony, Grace immediately concluded that her romance with the young curate was doomed. The crude threat had worked. For Grace it was unthinkable that her father might not be beside her in church, proud to be giving her away. Peter was dropped. The Reverend had imposed his will on Grace once again. But when would she wake to the truth that he had not the slightest intention of relinquishing her to another man; that he would never do so – not if he could help it.

Indeed, the Reverend was harbouring a strange fantasy of possession which had played on his mind for some time. He had a habit of using car journeys to talk openly with Grace about any one of a variety of intimate subjects. Often the topic was the deep pain he felt at not having had a child of his own – 'the greatest tragedy of my life,' as he invariably described it. But he had something else on his mind one day as he was driving twenty-four-year-old Grace from his curate's house in the Croydon diocese to Farnborough Hospital in Kent, where she was being trained in midwifery.

'Grace,' the reverend said rather tentatively. 'You know, I would love it if we could be together.'

'Yes, Daddy,' replied Grace, desperate to be back in the safety of the nurses' home.

'You know. I mean married. Why don't we just drive off somewhere now?'

'But you know that's impossible, Daddy.'

That matter-of-fact response may or may not have dispelled the bizarre fantasy from the Reverend's mind altogether, but Grace received no such proposals of marriage again.

As Grace approached her thirties, trapped as she was, she was becoming desperately tired of colluding in her father's tricks. Aware that their geographical separation had made no difference at all to his ability to control her, she resolved that in future she would try a different tack. If only she could keep her relationships secret, she reasoned, then he would have nothing to be upset about. His ignorance would be her bliss. And so began a gradual process of alienation from her parents that would come to characterize their relationship for many years. Birthdays and anniversaries were remembered, and there would be a polite exchange of cards and presents at Christmas. Underneath this semblance of normality there was no longer any real contact.

So when in 1964 Grace, who was now working as a health visitor in the Birmingham suburb of Erdington, met Alan

Stocken, an engineer, at a party in the city, she decided not to announce the news to her parents for the time being. In fact, Grace was to hold her tongue much longer than she expected, but for quite another reason. The courtship went on so long that she began to wonder whether Alan had any intention of ever proposing to her. When finally he did so, Grace gladly accepted and presented the couple's decision to the Manns as a *fait accompli*. For the first time in her life Grace had outwitted her father. The Reverend, realizing this, telephoned his daughter some six weeks before the wedding to make just one enquiry. It seemed as if he was already reconciled to her loss.

'You really are going to go through with this then, Grace? Then you really do want me to phone the Bishop?' he asked. Rather than a promise to engage the cleric's services, the question concealed a threat. The Reverend only had to tell the Bishop that as a non-practising Christian the young man was unsuitable as a husband for Grace to make it impossible for them to marry in that diocese.

Alarmed as she was by this possibility, Grace nevertheless replied in the affirmative. Indeed, so undaunted must she have sounded that at last the Reverend realized he was wasting his time contesting the match. In truth he was rather relieved that she had chosen someone well removed from Church circles, even though this was counter to everything that he had preached about the value of a shared religion. Even so, he decided to play one last desperate card. Aware of his daughter's medical history and of the surgeon's remarks after removing an ovarian cyst from her, he turned his attention to his prospective son-in-law. 'You do know,' he informed him, 'that Grace will never be able to have any children?' It was a malicious but futile manoeuvre, for Alan Stocken had already made up his mind: Grace was to be his wife.

Irene, sensing that her husband was downcast at the prospect of parting with his most prized possession, wondered if she might not be able to console him in some way. 'Is Alan taller than your father, Grace?' she asked the bride-to-be as she hung out the washing in her usual neat rows. Her mind on other things, Grace said she thought no, probably not. 'Good, good,' said her mother, aware that if there was little else to console him, here was a crumb of comfort for which the Reverend would be grateful.

In her own way Grace, too, sought to soften the blow for her father – not least because, if she went along with most of his wishes concerning the wedding, she felt he was less likely to engage in some last-minute manoeuvring calculated to prevent the wedding from taking place. Among his requests was to have a professional photograph of her before the fateful day. 'Grace, I want one last memory of you,' he explained solemnly, as if his daughter were about to disappear not just from his house but from the world. Even his wife remarked that it all seemed rather unnecessary. Nevertheless Grace agreed, and at the appointed time she presented herself in her father's study, dressed appropriately for the photographer. As it turned out, the session was a failure, for in her own words Grace looked 'strained, plump and matronly'. To her great relief, the portrait never found a place on the Manns' mantelpiece.

To Alan Stocken, entering his in-laws' world was a strange experience. His view of his prospective father-in-law was no doubt coloured by the fact that the Reverend grew ever gloomier as the wedding day approached. But even so, 'Edward Mann was like an alien from the moon to me,' he later said.

> He was a completely different sort of human being. I had no idea how to talk to him. His whole background was different to mine. He was steeped in the Church. Most of the discussion was based around marriages and deaths in his church – and I

found the whole set-up difficult to deal with. In fact, on the occasions when we did visit there would be these huge rows, often with tears, all in this highly charged emotional atmosphere. I had no idea what it was about. Recriminations would fly this way and that, and I found it all most unsettling. I used to breathe the most almighty sigh of relief as we drove off. I'm someone who just likes a quiet life.

When Grace opened her eyes on the morning of her wedding day, 10 December 1966, she felt a vague excitement, but at the same time there weighed upon her a sense of oppression that she knew would lift only when she was on her way to London for her honeymoon. Later, as she descended the stairs wearing her bridal dress and with her hair arranged, the Reverend studied her without a word, and he remained silent as they were driven the short distance from the rectory to St Mary's Parish Church, East Leake, Nottinghamshire.

The Lord Bishop of Southwell, the Right Reverend Gordon D. Savage, was waiting at the church door to usher in the wedding party. As the Reverend Mann escorted his daughter down the aisle the organist played a hymn that to Grace, in her excitement and anxiety, seemed strangely inappropriate. She swallowed hard on seeing her sister but gathered all her resolve to see the ceremony through. Before long the bells were ringing out joyously to celebrate the joining in holy matrimony of Grace Elizabeth Mann and Alan Stocken. The bride had every reason to be proud, for not only did she look radiant in her white wedding dress but it was the first time in her life that she had felt officially free. She could not believe her good fortune as Alan stood devotedly beside her. She had escaped the brutality of Nazi Germany at the tender age of three. Now, twenty-seven years later, she had finally escaped another form of tyranny, one fuelled by a fierce love which had gone beyond all acceptable bounds and which had suffocated her for years. Finally Grace could breathe the fresh air of freedom. For all that, it was not a day that she or Alan cared to reminisce about as the years went by, for the strain on them, not to mention the Reverend Mann, had been very great.

When, some weeks later, the proofs of the wedding photographs arrived, one person stood out as rather miserable, looking as gloomy as the weather on that overcast Saturday afternoon. Not surprisingly, it was the bride's father.

Ten months later a baby boy was born. James Frederick Stocken, he was to be christened.

'Don't you think he looks like Alan's mother?' Grace asked her father. To her mind, the boy's faintly ginger hair and the shape of the chin certainly recalled his paternal grandmother.

'How could you say that, Grace,' the Reverend replied, 'when you realize that I am childless?' He then added one of his passing observations on humanity in general: 'Isn't it strange, Grace, how the wicked people in this world always seem to get what they want?' So preoccupied was the Reverend with his own thwarted paternity that it drove out all thought for Grace at what was for her a very special time.

For two days after giving birth, Grace remained in a state of joy. What she did not know during that brief euphoria was that she was heading for the most enormous fall. The truth was that she had not planned to have a baby. Indeed she had been informed that she would have the greatest difficulty in becoming pregnant at all. Yet Grace had conceived within a month of her wedding. For her, it had happened much too quickly. All she had wanted was a little time to savour her freedom, to begin to relax at last.

Friends showed little sympathy, feeling that Grace scarcely had cause for complaint. A fully qualified health-care professional dedicated to her work, she had a kind, considerate husband and a home of her own. And now, just a few weeks before Christmas, she had been blessed with the gift of a healthy baby boy. But Grace was unable to respond with the instinctive happiness of many new mothers, for the birth had touched off all of the painful feelings associated with her own childhood.

Although it was to be some years yet before she would articulate it, she was struggling not just for uncomplicated fatherly approval, which had eluded her for so long, but for her mother's love too, for that had likewise been denied her. Suddenly the traumas of the past seemed to seize hold of her. Now a mother herself, she began to ponder the fate of her real parents. And what was the truth about the Munich orphanage? Had it really been burned to the ground and all the records destroyed, as she had been told?

With her hormones propelling her into in ever deeper depression, so that she was unable even to hold her new-born son, she had the good sense to know that she was in urgent need of help. Within a few weeks of returning home with her baby, Grace asked to be admitted as a voluntary patient to Birmingham's Highcroft Hospital, which she thought might provide a refuge. Just as her father before her, she too found herself in hospital on the brink of collapse. No, Grace Stocken, it seemed, had not found her freedom after all.

FIVE

Searching

When Grace resumed her role as mother and wife after a six-week spell in hospital, the more perceptive of her friends knew that the process of healing had still to run its course. They struggled to pinpoint the source of her malaise, for – despite Grace's protestations to the contrary – there was no doubt that all was far from well. As one of her friends observed:

> There always seemed to me to be something about Grace.
> Something that wasn't quite right. She didn't talk about
> herself very readily. There was a sort of vacuum, I suppose.

If there was indeed a vacuum, then Grace chose to fill it very skilfully. It was not long before, settled into married life in the small Warwickshire town of Rugby, she returned to full-time nursing, as a casualty sister in the accident and emergency department of the town's St Cross hospital.

Denial was the name of the game, a game Grace had been playing and would continue to play for a good many years. It was all part of a strategy for appearing as normal as the next person while knowing she was not. Deep down within her she could sense an ominous message whose full significance would not become clear until much later. 'But you don't really know who you are,' it would repeatedly remind her. Her busy life helped her to brush aside this thought, but, assuming she wanted to, where would she start if she did embark on that quest? In any case, was it not inevitable that the Reverend Mann would frustrate her efforts if she tried to search out the truth about her origins, just as he had controlled almost every other aspect of her life? Might there not be dread reprisals in store if she incurred his wrath once more? This was certainly Grace's childlike fear.

Instead she became an expert in covering up the identity she knew still lived somewhere inside her.

> Putting on a nurse's uniform was in effect putting on a mask. And I soon discovered that the mask of being a nurse was much more comfortable than having to be myself. In terms of mothering I didn't show much nurturing instinct; nor did I feel that I had found my feet as a wife. So nursing seemed to provide the answer for me. I just kept myself busy.

Within a few years, with her son away as a boarder at Southwell Minster Choir School in Nottinghamshire, and Alan working long days as a design engineer – on the luxury liner *QE2*, among other projects – Grace could devote most of her energies to nursing. She won praise from her superiors as a competent administrator and enjoyed a reputation for her highly conscientious approach to the job – so much so that in time she was promoted to the position of nursing sister.

The mask Grace had adopted did not slip for nearly two decades. However, during her thirties and forties this constant concealment was to exact a price: the gradual destruction of her mental and physical health until she was very fragile indeed. The mask was becoming less and less comfortable.

If Grace had long succeeded in shielding herself from her past, the sense of loss that this entailed was brought home to her most poignantly when she was thirty-five. For that is when Eunice died, at a Cheshire Home for young chronically ill patients, after bravely clinging to life for many years. With her sister's death went Grace's last link with a past that the Manns had striven to bury for decades. But, far from consigning her early years to oblivion, this loss fuelled the need that she felt growing ever more urgent within her to reclaim her roots.

In 1985, when she was forty-nine, Grace herself fell ill. A hysterectomy went smoothly enough, but psychologically the outcome was far from satisfactory. Grace's underlying depression, which her unstinting dedication to her work had kept at bay for so many years, returned with a vengeance, and once again she found herself plunging into a dark spiral of despair. Desperate for help and feeling that conventional medicine had little to offer beside pills, she turned first to meditation to bring relaxation, and then to prayer. Both provided moments of relief but failed to tackle the underlying problem. The answer lay within:

> I finally realized that in order to recover and proceed with life I needed to know who I was. It was as simple as that. Not knowing was a dark cloud that hung over me and this affected the whole way I operated. Because not knowing who your real parents are means that you have nothing at all to hang on to. It's like being on a raft in the middle of the ocean – you are drifting, there is no anchor, you just don't know where you have come from. I always knew that one day I would have to face up to this. But I always managed to find an excuse to put that day off. It all seemed too exhausting. Could I settle for nothing at the end of a long search? It was a question I couldn't answer until I knew I was ready to face any consequences.

As if preparing herself for the great quest which over the next few years would come close to being an obsession, Grace suggested that a touring holiday in Europe with friends might assist her recovery. As they were driving through

Munich in the summer of 1985, on an impulse she asked Alan to stop at a public phone booth. They were in the birthplace of her and her twin sister – and, she was chillingly aware, of the whole Nazi movement. Grace got out of the car and began scanning the local telephone directory for the name Bechhöfer, the surname she had been obliged to use on her exam papers some thirty years earlier.

Not a single person with that name was listed. This came as no surprise to Grace. But then, having grown up in a household where she was forbidden to read newspapers or magazines, where the radio was seldom turned on, and where discussion of the recent past was strenuously discouraged, she had remained largely ignorant of the destruction of Germany's Jews and indeed of the monstrous legacy of the Holocaust. The first spontaneous move in her quest had been fruitless, and two more years were to pass before it was truly under way.

Part of the reason for this delay was the fact that Grace had been told that all documentation relating to her origins had been destroyed. There was simply very little to go on. All she knew was that at the age of three she and Eunice had come to Britain from a Munich orphanage which had soon after burned down, with the loss of all its records. The risk of disappointment in delving into such a murky past also seemed too great. Finally, but by no means the least of her reasons for not embarking on her search, was the fact that Grace was still nervous about what the Reverend Mann's reaction might be on learning of her project. She may have reached middle age but her emotions were still in turmoil from having suffered for so long from one man's obsessive control of her.

When, in 1987, after nearly thirty years in the profession, Grace retired from nursing, she suddenly found time weighing heavily on her. There was no longer a hospital ward to run. Nor were there many domestic duties to attend to, for her son, who by this time preferred to be known by his middle name, Frederick, had won a place as an organ scholar at Cambridge. Aware of the need to occupy her mind, and keen to pursue her artistic impulses, Grace joined a creative writing class run by Rugby District Council. It was there that she became friendly with Hazel Bell, also a Rugby housewife, with whom Grace found she had something in common. Hazel Bell had problems of her own and one evening spoke at length about them to her new friend, for Grace had become an accomplished listener. But as they chatted into the small hours it became clear that Hazel expected Grace to reveal a little of herself in return. 'Why is it, Grace,' she asked, 'that I can't seem to get close to you? Why is it you put up so many barriers and don't seem prepared to let anyone in?'

Never before had Grace been challenged so directly. Alarm bells began to sound in her mind: the great secret, kept under wraps for so many years, was under attack. Unsure of just how much she should reveal to placate her friend, she told her that it was extremely difficult for her to communicate properly with people because she did not know much about her own identity. For this reason it had always been easier to listen than to talk.

But Hazel was clearly determined to draw her friend out. In reply, Grace explained that she and Eunice had come to Britain from an orphanage in Germany the day after their third birthday, but that she knew little more. Repeating a refrain familiar since her childhood, she described how the issue of her identity had always been shrouded in the greatest secrecy, hastily adding that she was quite unused to telling people about it. Even her husband knew precious little about her past. It had always seemed wiser to say nothing at all.

Hazel was intrigued; the creative writing course had never furnished such fascinating material. But Grace insisted that there was nothing else she could say: 'Because I simply don't know any more.'

As tenacious and clear-sighted as any lawyer cross-examining a defendant, Hazel persisted, eventually throwing down the gauntlet. 'Grace,' she said, ' why don't you see if you can find out who you are?'

Her own imagination now fired by the prospect of finding her real parents, Grace cast her remaining doubts aside. She knew she had exhausted all the excuses which had served her so faithfully over the years. Now the friendly helping hand of Hazel Bell was extended to her, and it was too good an offer to refuse. Nearly fifty years after her departure from Munich as a orphaned toddler, she had the green light.

After a few hours' sleep things looked rather different, however. Grace was still strongly motivated, yet in the cold light of day she felt she had not the faintest prospect of finding out anything about her natural parents, and thus her own identity. After all, the Munich orphanage, like the absence of Bechhöfers in the city, was surely a closed book.

On the other hand, Grace was lucky that the legislation on issues of adoption had been moving in her favour. The Children Act of 1975 had made important changes in the law relating to access to birth records. Adults who had been adopted were now able to apply to see the original documents. This was a radical shift from earlier government policy, for previously it had been judged best for an adopted child's break with the past to be total. One sentence from a leaflet published by Her Majesty's Stationery Office described the situation succinctly: 'It is now recognized that although adoption makes a child a full member of a new family, information about his origins may still be important to him.'

This development above all else helped dispel Grace's hesitation, for she realized that information about her birth was not just important – it was the key to her hidden past.

The bit firmly between her teeth again, she told herself that many years had been wasted and there was no time to lose.

For those adopted before 12 November 1975, when the new legislation came into force, it had become obligatory to see a social worker trained in counselling. This consultation would help the adopted person to understand the many regulations and procedures surrounding adoption, as well as the possible results of his or her enquiries. Bureaucracy beckoned.

On 17 January 1988, Grace travelled to Warwick to meet Bert Cuff, a social worker whose open smile seem to convey what she had been hoping for. Although helpful and sympathetic, he was at first frankly sceptical about his client's chances of success. Aware that to raise false expectations was to risk doing great damage, he adopted a very cautious approach. 'Mrs Stocken,' he explained, 'it's been fifty years. After fifty years it really is very unlikely that you are going to get anywhere at all.'

'But I've really got to try,' Grace replied through her tears. 'I really feel as if this is something that I've got to do. And all the more so now because I've waited so long before trying to find out.'

Bert Cuff did not need much persuading. Sensing his client's determination and identifying with her plight, he soon became a true ally. He said he was sure that Grace was mature enough to proceed – for that was the judgement the law required him to make – and in addition promised he would do all in his power to help. 'Your first move must be to write to the District Registry of the High Court of Justice at Croydon County Court, in order to obtain your birth certificate,' he explained.

It was not until the twins were nineteen that the Manns had succeeded in adopting them, their formal adoption having taken place at the law courts in Croydon, Surrey. Until that time Grace and Eunice had been fostered. The

Jewish Refugees Committee of the Central British Fund had ruled, at the time of their fostering, that before adoption took place each child must be at least eighteen years old and that it must be the wish of the adoptee.

Grace was ignorant of these conditions – she had always believed that she and Eunice had been adopted from the start. In fact, when Eunice was nineteen the Manns thought that her end could not be far away, because she was deteriorating fast. For the Reverend, who had always done his utmost to conceal everything related to the twins' past, it would have been unthinkable to bury his daughter as Lotte Bechhöfer, the name given to her at birth. This dread prospect explains his haste formally to adopt her.

The Chief Clerk at Croydon County Court came back to Grace with a disappointing reply: the court held no copies of any birth certificates, and so it would be necessary to enquire elsewhere. In fact, Grace was already busy writing and dispatching letters daily, including one to the German Consulate in London. As usual, she had outlined the few facts she knew about herself in the hope that these were enough to make a proper investigation possible.

Alan Stocken had his reservations about the wisdom of his wife's quest. Seldom did a day go by, he noticed, without Grace sending off a letter to this authority or that. She was spending more and more time alone in her study on the first floor of their house planning her strategy. Was there any real point, he wondered, in attempting to delve into the past? And most worrying of all, was it not extremely likely that his wife would be hurt and disappointed, and therefore even more damaged, as she pursued her single-minded goal? Suspecting that trying to uncover one's roots could prove a risky business, he was anxious to replace the lid on that particular Pandora's box. Not that his misgivings would have made the slightest difference, for Grace was now a woman who could not be diverted from her mission, as Alan would later explain:

74

Grace knows her own mind. Right from square one she
wanted to pursue this. So I wasn't going to dissuade her,
because I thought it might make her a fuller person. She has
had her difficulties in the past, probably because she didn't
have a settled family life, so I was worried that attempting to
find out things might be quite traumatic. And there was a time
when this search seemed to take her over completely – and it
began to pull us apart. But there was nothing I could do to
prevent her from taking the path she was taking.

Nor did Frederick offer much support, for he had worries
of his own, in particular his studies at Cambridge. Indeed he
shared his father's reservations. As a result, Grace's only
active ally at this time was Hazel Bell. As Grace's initial file
began to swell, the two women began to fantasize about the
identity of Grace's real parents. Inspired by their writing
course, together they concocted a Mills-&-Boon-style
romance. As they saw it, describing the passionate liaison
between Grace's mother and her father was the ultimate creative writing challenge.

'We would have this wonderful romantic story about two
people coming together under the clouds of war,' Hazel
recalls. 'Grace was convinced that this was a fairly educated
background as far as her mother was concerned. I used to
say, "What about father, though?" Together we built up a
picture of this gay, abandoned, swashbuckling, rather handsome sort of guy.'

Fortunately, others were more concerned with the facts,
notably the German Consulate, which seemed to be devoting
a good deal of time to its research. In the summer of 1988,
four months after Grace had written, she received the
Consulate's reply. Suddenly and unexpectedly there had been
a breakthrough. Researchers in Germany had unearthed
Grace's birth certificate. Not only that: they had sent her
the original. She was indeed Susi Bechhöfer, born in Munich
on 17 May 1936. Welcome as it was, that information merely

75

confirmed what she already knew. But then, casting her eyes to the bottom of the document, she saw the names of both her parents for the first time. Of course, two surnames could mean only one thing: that her parents were not married. Not that Grace cared: the crucial thing had been to establish their identity, and that much she had achieved. Her diary recalls her elation that day:

> I'm walking on air, I really am. It's a fragment really, but it means an awful lot to me. My father has a name. And my mother has a name too. For the first time that makes them real people. I feel as if I have found something out. I've never seen their names before – it's just wonderful.

The document also revealed that Rosa Bechhöfer was born in Ansbach in Germany on 7 July 1898. But no additional information had been found about Otto Hald, her father. Was this just the start of a journey of discovery? Or would the spring in her step turn into a stumble, she wondered, and then a fall? But, as she pondered her next move, there was really only one question in her mind: whatever had become of Rosa and Otto?

PART II
Towards the Light

SIX

Rosa

During the summer of 1988 Bertha Leverton was working flat out. In under nine months' time her detailed plans and preparations were to be put to the test. The fiftieth anniversary of the Kindertransport was approaching fast, and she was determined that the occasion of the mass exodus of Jewish children from Germany, Austria, Czechoslovakia and Poland should not go unnoticed. It was not a case of generating publicity for publicity's sake; far from it. She had a precise purpose in mind. Having left Munich with her younger sister at the age of fifteen, Bertha's mission in life – for that is what it had become – was to compile a register of names and addresses so that the former children of the transports, now mostly middle-aged or elderly, might be able to get in touch, not just with one another, but also any surviving family members or friends.

It was Bertha's fervent hope that a book of individual reminiscences might also be compiled after the reunion, so that Gentiles and Jews alike might be less inclined to close their minds to the atrocities of the recent past. Of course the Holocaust was a fact, she would often affirm, but that did not mean that crumbs of comfort could not be picked up here and there. She might well have failed to convince some of her friends, many of whom preferred to dwell on less weighty issues, of the value of her mission, but she had persuaded the BBC to give her a hearing. So, before long her message, together with her own poignant story of separation and struggle, was being broadcast to millions of radio listeners on *Woman's Hour*.

Grace Stocken happened to be tuned to Radio Four that day, and as she listened to Bertha Leverton speak about the forthcoming Kindertransport reunion she felt that here might be a key capable of unlocking a number of important doors for her. She had managed to obtain her birth certificate, true enough, but there had been very little progress since then. Noticing that the date and circumstances of her own flight from Germany tallied with those mentioned on the programme, she began to suspect that she herself had been one of the Kinder.

As soon as the programme was over she wrote to Bertha at the address in Stanmore, north-west London, which the BBC had given out to listeners. 'I too am a survivor – brought over from Munich in May 1939,' she explained. 'It is with regret that I have never known anything of my real parentage and am only now attempting to make some kind of contact.'

'I had had many letters,' Bertha would later explain, 'but when I got to Grace's I felt very emotional – something told me that there was something special and that I had to do my utmost to help. I myself came from Munich, so I felt a special kinship with her – and it went straight to my heart.' Bertha replied by return of post:

> Your letter suggests that you must have been very young when you came, to have no memories of your childhood days. Among my friends there are several who came from Munich and perhaps between us, if we know your maiden name, we might be able to help. I can think of many ways for you to get in touch with people, but it will take some time...

Grace was delighted to have found a new ally in her cause. Here was someone who was not only prepared to take her seriously, but who apparently also wanted to establish a number of further particulars about her case. With a response like this Grace needed no prompting to take up Bertha's offer of help. Within a week of the broadcast she was writing a second letter to Bertha.

At the start of this year I started the ball rolling and six weeks ago I received my original birth certificate. After 52 years I now know who my father and mother were (names only). I was one of twins. We were both brought over and resided (somewhat unhappily) with a family in Wales. My sister died at the age of 35 yrs (tumour on the brain). Since 19 yrs I have devoted my life to nursing and have just recently retired. I tell you these facts briefly in order that we get to know each other. At last I feel I have a 'link'. I am thank God happily married with one son who is extraordinarily gifted as a musician. He is an organ scholar in Cambridge. Hopes to compose and conduct as a career. Am certain he will! It is he alone that I have but maybe there are blood ties somewhere? Can you help me?

It is a slightly unusual situation. My father's name was Otto Hald. My mother's name was Rosa Bechhöfer. I was Susi Bechhöfer. My sister was Lotte Bechhöfer. Born 17.5.1936 in Munich. We were brought over I am told from an orphanage in 1939, which burned to the ground 3 weeks later. I only tell you this as every clue might help. I have been wondering what to do next. Can you advise me? Please only when you have time and put this letter to the bottom of your large pile!

Bertha had no intention of putting Grace's letter at the bottom of her pile, and once again interrupted her many administrative tasks connected with the reunion to reply at once.

You are certainly not a nuisance and I don't think you are the only one either who is in the same position – but personally I have not come across any other stories like yours. My sister

81

who was 8 at the time came across with a later transport and remembers a baby of about 10 months and a little girl of two on her train from Munich.

At least you have established your name and have your birth certificate. I am enclosing information for 2 things you could try. First of all the C.B.F. has or had records of all children who had arrived at that time. I recently found that out by chance and sent for my record. But they did tell me that some got lost during the war. It's worth a try though. Secondly, I enclose a monthly paper printed in London. You could write a letter to them asking any people who came from Munich and who remember your family to contact you. There are also several German Jewish Old Age homes in London and some of their residents may be able to remember your parents. I suggest you get a duplicate letter and send it to the matron of each home. But get it typed in the largest clearest print, as handwriting is very hard to read.

If you are adventurous you could even try the BBC unit, the name escapes me for the moment, who take such a challenge worldwide if their imagination is fired. Actually BBC television told me yesterday that they will be putting this over as a major event. If you like I could interest them in your story. But you must realize that should they take it on, they would make big news of it and you would become known and so would your history. Now I would go all out were it me, but I realize that some people would be reluctant to become news. Not that anyone can promise the outcome or if they would do it. But in conjunction with a 50 year event it might help. Anyway, it's up to you. I will gladly help if I can.

In suggesting to Grace that she make contact with the CBF – the Central British Fund for World Jewish Relief – Bertha had indeed given her the best possible advice. For there in London, among the Jewish Refugees Archives, were a number of papers which gave details of the Antonienheim orphanage where the twins had been left by their mother. There too, locked away in filing cabinets or sitting on shelves gathering dust as the years slipped by, were the documents which had allowed Susi and Lotte Bechhöfer to enter England.

Deprived for the best part of fifty years of any scrap of information about her origins, merely to learn of the existence of these files was an overwhelming experience for Grace. How many times had she been told that they had been destroyed by fire? Evidently that was not true. Not that the CBF was in a hurry to release the documents. Grace's request would have to be considered by a meeting of the full committee.

Major upheavals were in prospect, and aware that she was in a fragile state, Grace embarked on a series of counselling sessions. Her best friend, however, remained her pen. Time and again she would turn to her diary for comfort and support. It was a method of self-help as effective as any therapeutic technique.

> Bertha, she is just amazing. Her commitment on my behalf is just staggering. I have heard the name Bechhöfer mentioned TWICE for the first time in my whole life. I feel exhilarated, confused, bemused, the timing of events is remarkable. Will they all be related? I must keep an open mind. I do believe I feel very special tonight. Events I feel may overtake me. I must keep calm and peaceful. My destiny surely has to be recorded. There is so much for me to learn. May I have the eyes and ears to know what is being told me. I need help. Someone who can listen and explore my true feelings…

The next day the diary revealed a mixture of hope and pain:

> I am beginning to become aware of vital links that have been troubling me – the cessation of mother bonding – her pain, my pain, the disorientation that so often surrounds and confuses me emotionally, my endless seeking and yearning, my nightmares, my fears. I feel as though I am gradually becoming grounded and experiencing a miracle – the meaning of my life is becoming clearer.

On the practical level, Grace's quest at this stage took the form of gathering information. While waiting for the CBF to reply to her request to inspect their files, she continued to write to a wide variety of individuals and organizations. She contacted the Red Cross in London and then the International Tracing Service of its international committee in Arolsen in Germany. She began corresponding with a number of old people's homes in London and Dublin. She wrote to the World Tracing Centre and the Association of Jewish Ex-Servicemen. Her strategy was simplicity itself: every opportunity must be seized, every contact pursued with the utmost vigour. In this spirit she sought the help of the Jews' Temporary Shelter in London, only to learn that not a single one of its branches, who all apologized with the greatest regret, could offer her any help in tracing her parents.

Many other letters were sent and received, and many phone calls made, and as the volume of both grew daily, so did the financial burden of Grace's mission. Every now and then, in between drafting and reading letters, in between hopes raised and hopes dashed, she would pause to question her own motivation. 'Why am I doing all this?' she asked her diary. 'Because I think it would be an understatement to say that Rosa's heart would be very warmed to know that all of this is happening. To think that I am retracing her steps. This is amazing. Fate has made this happen, together with the help of other people like Bertha and the BBC.'

As a small child she had had no say in the matter, of course, but the fact remained that Grace had been brought up within the framework of Christianity. Her foster father had earned his living first as a Baptist minister then as a vicar in the Church of England, so it could not have been otherwise. Her whole life had been spent far from the big cities of Britain where Jewish life has long flourished and still remains strong: places like London, Manchester and Leeds. In fact, Bertha Leverton was the first Jew with whom Grace had ever knowingly been in contact, or at least since her departure from the Antonienheim at the age of three.

And yet the idea that she herself might be a Jew was now beginning to sink in. Deprived as she had been of knowledge of her own past and of the fate of Europe's Jewry, the possibility had not occurred to Grace before. Not even when she heard Bertha Leverton speak on the radio about the Kindertransport did the idea suggest itself, even though she felt a strangely close kinship with those children. It was not until she had made contact with Bertha and felt, through her letters, the woman's assurance and sincerity, that the seed took root in her mind. Whether consciously or not, Bertha gave not a second thought to any other possibility. Rather she built up a case for Grace's being Jewish with her casual references to the *Jewish Chronicle* and the Central Jewish Board, and her proposal to ask all her Jewish friends if they knew anyone with the name Bechhöfer.

Hazel Bell, the friend in Rugby who had gone out of her way to encourage Grace to embark on the search for her past, was likewise aware of the possibility that Grace might be Jewish.

Suddenly you have a Christian lady, whose son plays the organ recitals from time to time in the parish church of St Andrew – and you have this sudden idea that she might be Jewish. And it caused quite a consternation with her – and with me too really. Because I had always regarded two of the things that she and I had always had in common were being English women – all right so that had been wiped out – she's not an English woman at all – she's German or at least basically so. And then the other thing – that we are both Christian ladies – well that's suddenly sent into touch as well because maybe she isn't. Maybe she's Jewish.

Of course, there was no maybe about it. For some time Bertha had been pointing out to Grace during their various telephone conversations that Bechhöfer was a distinctly

Jewish name. In fact she was quite wrong. 'Bechhöfer' was a perfectly typical, though not at all common, German name, simply implying that its bearers' ancestors came from a place called Bechhof or Bechhofen. Hundreds of Germans, Austrians and Swiss surnames are similarly linked to locations. While it is true that most German names found in Britain belong to Jews, there was nothing distinctly Jewish about Bechhöfer. Nevertheless, right or wrong in the basis of her analysis, Bertha had clearly planted a fertile seed in Grace's mind. Here was a notion that Grace Stocken, Christian, churchgoer and long-time subscriber to the *Church Times*, was quite unable to digest. She was hardly aware of the existence of a Jewish community in England, let alone acquainted with its customs and beliefs.

'I didn't know what "kosher" meant,' Grace recalls. 'Seder night and so on – it all meant nothing to me. As far as I was concerned, Jews were people who lived in the East End of London. They were tailors who had gone on to make a lot of money.'

Bertha again suggested that Grace should apply to the Central British Fund in London for documentation on her and her twin sister. She was convinced that there would be a record of their having come to Britain on one of the Kindertransports. And, because the organization was sure to hold a record of their having been fostered, there might also be more about their earliest years – and perhaps about their mother. The CBF requested that Grace travel to London, since such matters were best dealt with in person. On a grey November morning Bertha met her from the train at Euston Station, and for the first time Grace saw the kind face that she had tried so often to imagine.

At the CBF Grace met the secretary of the Jewish Refugees Committee, Heather Salmon, whose pleasant and assured manner put her at her ease from the start, despite the difficult nature of what they were there to discuss.

ABOVE. Rosa Bechhöfer, the penniless, unskilled and unmarried Jewish mother, was desperate to save her children from an unknown fate under the Nazis.

RIGHT. Otto Hald was a great womanizer. Whilst the nature of his affair with Rosa remains unclear, he did not hesitate to abandon her upon discovering she was pregnant with his twins.

ABOVE. The Antonienheim Jewish orphanage in Munich was the first home for Rosa's children. She visited Susi and Lotte regularly on her days off as a housemaid.

BELOW LEFT. This photograph of Susi and Lotte's first birthday at the Antonienheim was discovered in Israel over fifty years later among the personal possessions of a former staff member.

BELOW RIGHT. The bewildered twins, too young to understand their fate, were taken from Liverpool Street Station to their new home in Wales by their foster parents, Reverend Edward Mann and his wife Irene.

Lfb. Nr.	Familien- und Vornamen, Familienstand, Beruf, Geburtszeit und -Gemeinde		Stod	Wohnt bei Nr.	Einzug			Auszug			Abgemeldet nach
					Tag	Monat	Jahr	Tag	Monat	Jahr	
315	Schapira	Josefine, Kind 26.10.34 Mehn.			15	9	36	28	9	36	Burgdorfstr. 1
316	Bechhöfer	Süsanne, Jüra 17.5.36 Mehn			9	9	36	16	5	39	England
317	Seidemann	Henny, Kind 6.11.22 Berlin			21	9	36	1	5	28	Grillparzerstr. 36
318	Bechhöfer	Lotte, Jüra 17.5.36 Mehn			9	9	36	16	5	39	England
319	Freimann	Ruth,			25	9	36	9	12	36	Beuthen

ABOVE. The records of the Antonienheim show Susi and Lotte Bechhöfer leaving the orphanage for England on 16 May 1939, three and a half months before the outbreak of the Second World War.

BELOW. Susi's entry permit to the UK was secured by the Central British Fund, a charitable organization attempting to secure the safe passage of Jewish children out of Nazi Germany.

58

This document of identity is issued with the approval of His Majesty's Government in the United Kingdom to young persons to be admitted to the United Kingdom for educational purposes under the care of the Inter-Aid Committee for children.

THIS DOCUMENT REQUIRES NO VISA.

N.T

PERSONAL PARTICULARS.

Name BECHHÖFER   SUSI

Sex FEMALE   Date of Birth 17.5.36.

Place MÜNCHEN

Full Names and Address of Parents

BECHHÖFER   OTTO & ROSA

7, ANTONIENSTR.

MÜNCHEN 23

The twins, now with new identities, adapted to their new British life protected by the care and concern of their new foster parents.

Irene Mann divided her time between bringing up the twins and carrying out duties within the Baptist Church. From the outset she bonded more closely with Lotte.

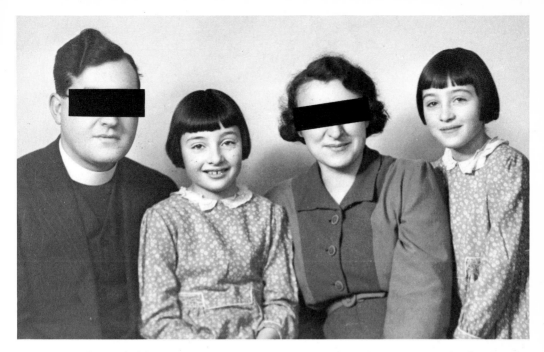

ABOVE. Their early life with the Reverend Mann and his wife was happy. It was only after the diagnosis of Lotte's tragic illness that Susi's life at home took a sinister turn.

BELOW. Susi (centre with glasses) at the Park School in Yeovil brooded over her relationships at home and resented the attention lavished on her sickly sister by Mrs Mann which left Susi at the mercy of the Reverend.

ABOVE. Lotte (seated centre), aged 22, received the Award for Fortitude in the face of her illness.

BELOW LEFT. It was only when Susi left home to train as a nurse that the enormity of the injustice she had suffered dawned on her.

BELOW RIGHT. Brigitte Hald, living in Munich, coincidentally shared the family name of Susi's natural father, Otto Hald. Moved by Susi's tale she vowed to help her search for her roots in Germany.

RIGHT. Martina Uhlitzsch, the final link to Susi's past, was discovered by Brigitte Hald living in Dresden.

BELOW. Jerry Bechhofer (far left with his family) living in New York was the relation unearthed by Susi's search. In a letter to her he asked 'So, are you our cousin? If so, are you not one of the twins?' When Susi wrote back he replied 'Of course you are our cousin ... It's very simple. Your mother was our Tante Rosel ...'

Susi Bechhöfer, a practising psychotherapist, now lives in Rugby. Pictured here with her husband Alan Stocken and son Frederick, Susi has laid to rest the events of her tragic life. But the memory of Rosa, the mother she never knew, will always be with her.

Heather indicated that there was unlikely to be any problem with the release of the papers and that the committee's formal approval was only a week or two away. However, before coming to the records themselves, she advised Grace that she should set aside time to study Judaism before meeting her new-found cousin and his extended orthodox-Jewish family. She then explained how the organization's records were compiled and stored, and that sadly in some cases material that had once been held was now lost. The details of the Manns' fostering of the Bechhöfer twins were there in the records, and particularly poignant for Grace were the claims that the couple made for financial assistance during the early days of Eunice's illness.

At one point in the meeting, as if in the distance, Grace heard Heather ask: 'Do I call you Grace or do I call you Susi?' Grace's immediate reaction was to reply: 'Grace, of course.' But then she paused, acutely aware of two things: first, she was not who she thought she was; second, she had a choice in the matter of her identity. 'Maybe Susi-Grace, in the circumstances,' she answered.

By the time she got home that evening she had made up her mind: Grace was to be abandoned without further delay. 'When Grace came in and announced that night that henceforth she wanted to be known as Susi, I just burst out laughing,' recalls Alan. 'I couldn't help it. Because I had become used to her mood swings, I assumed this was just another one. I did know that she never liked the name Grace though. So I thought that the best thing to do would be for me to call her "dear". I find that's the easiest way out for me.' In fact Alan did not really mind Grace becoming Susi; it was the possibility of his wife's adoption of the alien-sounding Bechhöfer, supplanting his own surname, that he objected to.

But for Susi the issue of names was just as serious, if for different reasons. If she could dispense with the name Grace, could she not jettison too the feelings that had troubled the

87

bearer of that name? In time she was able to convince Alan that she had no alternative, and that adopting a new name, strange and springing from nowhere as it seemed, was an essential part of reclaiming the identity she had lost.

Now, as throughout his wife's search for herself, Alan provided the support she desperately needed. Loyal throughout the years of Susi's quest, he possessed a calm objectivity that was the perfect foil to her occasional overenthusiasm. He could stand back and tell her candidly what he thought, but she knew that whether or not he agreed with her latest line of enquiry he would not impede her, far less pass judgement.

As the preparations for the Kindertransport reunion continued apace Bertha was contacted by Sally George, a talented television producer working for the BBC. Sally had been commissioned to produce a documentary about the Kindertransport movement. Her provisional title was 'No Time To Say Goodbye', a phrase which, although not conceived with the Bechhöfer family in mind, could not have been more apt. Bertha insisted that Sally and Susi should meet, convinced that here was a story to capture the imagination of the public.

Susi was currently engaged in some additional research, but it was hardly the stuff of television documentaries. As usual, her approach was to gather information assiduously. How else could she evaluate the religion into which she had been born? Setting aside a couple of hours a day for study, she worked her way through a pile of books with titles like *A Dictionary of Judaism* and *Being Jewish*. What Susi was learning about the Jewish identity and experience was bringing about a revolution in her feelings. The Kindertransport story, for example, proved an eye-opening lesson in her personal history and that of the Jews. It was also an extremely painful one, but who better to confide in than her diary?

I am walking down the corridors of childhood again. I've got to recapture this childhood I was denied; my Jewishness, my heritage too. We Kindertransport children have carried invisible labels around our necks for fifty years. Only now are we being recognized. Of course it must have taken courage to put us on the trains and boats. But the screams still echo in our hearts today.

On 13 October 1988 Susi was to issue a scream of an altogether different kind – one of unrestrained joy. It was on that day that she received the information about her mother for which she had been waiting so patiently. Heather Salmon had now reviewed the files and wrote to Susi: 'We have been able to find a few record sheets and registration cards in our archives relating to yourself, your late twin sister Lotte and your mother, Rosa Bechhöfer, who came to England as a domestic servant, though the date of her arrival in this country is unknown.'

Susi would later recall that on that day:

I was just staggered that she could possibly be in this
country. And I worked out that she'd be ninety or ninety-one.
I thought that meant that she was unlikely to be alive – but
that there was a chance. So I felt this most enormous sense of
urgency to do whatever I could to find her. I was also thrilled
to think that she would have avoided being sent to a concentration camp, because that eventuality had always been at the
back of my mind. That meant everything to me. I felt that I
knew precisely what had happened. She had somehow managed to escape from the Nazis and come to this country in
order to find her daughters. Perhaps she been unable to find
us because we had had our names changed.

Given a massive boost in resolve by this breakthrough, Susi redoubled her efforts and telephoned every single Jewish old people's home in the country. In each case, after apologizing for being a nuisance she would simply state that she was trying to track down an elderly woman by the name of

Rosa Bechhöfer. She would then furnish the few facts she had been able to learn about her mother. But it was all to no avail. No one had ever heard of her.

Undaunted, Susi contacted the Domestic Services Visa Department of the Home Office in London, which had processed the relevant applications in the first instance. She cited the reference number and date of her mother's visa application by the Home Office – DOM 36572, 30 April 1943 – information now available to her thanks to the release of the CBF documents. Although Susi knew that the date referred to the day the Home Office recorded receipt of the document, rather than the date on which Rosa had dispatched her application, she felt sure that those facts would give the bureaucrats something concrete to work on.

Susi's hopes soared on receiving confirmation that the British government was still processing such applications in the spring of 1943. But still there was no trace of Rosa Bechhöfer.

SEVEN

Otto

Otto Hald was never more at ease than when he was in his workshop. There he would spend hours meticulously analysing one metallic substance before rejecting it in favour of another, all the time wondering if he would one day strike lucky by inventing a substance which he could patent and promote. An unlikely combination, Otto's three great passions were wine, women and welding.

Rosa Bechhöfer was but one of the large number of women with whom Otto had become involved. Ever since his hasty departure from Munich in early 1936, in the fifth month of her pregnancy, he had done his utmost to put both her plight and his guilt out of his mind – not always successfully.

Otto himself had not had an easy childhood. The youngest of four children, he was only ten when his mother, Mathilde Hald, died. He might have had time to adjust to that tragic blow had not his father remarried so soon afterwards. As it was, within a year Otto found himself in a strained relationship with a forty-year-old stepmother. But if all this had led to any instability in Otto, he disguised it well, for by the time he was in his teens he was an effective communicator, and he grew up cultivating the image of a creative person effortlessly exuding great confidence; an outgoing, dynamic personality with a healthy appetite for life.

A few years later Otto would need no reminding that to many women he was very attractive indeed. His attraction lay just as much in his sparkling wit and easy banter as in his dark, swarthy good looks and his penetrating brown eyes. Nor did the fact that his version of events was often at odds with reality seem to deter his admirers. The elderly Gertrud May, from Göppingen, where Otto was born, contacted BBC researchers after they advertised for information on Susi's father. Possibly the only person still living who knew him, she gave the lie to the impression Otto gave of being from a wealthy family, although she did not deny his success with women:

> He was a Casanova! Always up to mischief. Always after the girls. That was his main hobby. Poor as a church mouse, but always talking big. Always showing off, yet none of it was true. Like boasting about a big factory. That kind of thing. You know: 'My father owns a big factory. I live in this grand place' – both of which were simply not true. He was a good-looking chap, though, a really handsome man. So the women chased him all right, but not half as much as he chased them.

Rosa Bechhöfer had fallen for Otto's undoubted charms. Once carrying his twins, however, she learned that their relationship, already outlawed by the Nazi legislation on mingling Aryan and Jewish blood, was to come to an abrupt end. She was also made painfully aware that her lover's behaviour was not as charming as she had once thought – not least because he could not even muster the courage to tell her face to face that it was all over. Instead he simply packed his bags and left Munich for pleasures new.

Later on, as a private in Hitler's army, Otto served the Führer faithfully, although like many Germans his heart was never in the war. Nor could its ravages diminish his enthusiasm for the opposite sex. During the autumn of 1942, just as the great turning points of the war were taking place at Stalingrad and El Alamein, he met Luisa Lehmann. Otto was twenty-eight, and Luisa some seven years younger.

The couple married in January 1943, but after six years Luisa could tolerate Otto's ways no more. Devoted to him as she undoubtedly was, his womanizing and drinking were too much to bear. He had ignored her desperate ultimatum and so she initiated a divorce. Unaccustomed to rejection, Otto sought solace not just in drink, a familiar enough refuge, but in the fact that the time he had spent experimenting in his workshop seemed at last to have paid off. For by the early 1950s, as Germany embarked on a period of rapid and sustained recovery after the devastation of the war, he was confident that he had concocted a welding substance second to none. He could hardly get to Leipzig's patent office quickly enough to register the product he called Sepa-Ha.

So successful was Otto's innovation that within two years of its arrival on the market he found himself with a problem he had never had to confront before: two massive tax demands. He had set aside no money at all for such an eventuality, and there was no way he could pay. Otto's solution to his problem had a familiar ring: during the early hours one morning he slipped out of Leipzig and made his way to West Germany. Never again, he vowed, would he return to the East. True to character, Otto invited his housekeeper to accompany him on his journey into the unknown, thus ensuring that his new life as a tax fugitive would not be too lonely. Having been his mistress for some years, she was more than happy to agree.

The couple settled in the town of Marl, in the Ruhr industrial district, where the combination of the many chemical factories and West Germany's soaring post-war economy kept Otto amply supplied with work. But, in one extravagant gesture after another, he soon frittered away the money he had earned from patenting Sepa-Ha. Nor had he given his ex-wife a single pfennig in maintenance, steadfastly refusing to pay.

It was in 1988 that Susi began her search for her father. She was not sure whether he was alive or dead – so far the only information she had been able to gather was his name. Unlike the dossier on her mother, which seemed to grow by the day, there was nothing at all on Otto Hald. It was precisely because she had so little hard information on her father that Susi continued to indulge in a string of romantic illusions about him and his relationship with Rosa. She noted in her diary as she was about to begin the search for her father:

> What I know instinctively is that it was a love affair. I think
> that they were very much in love and it was partly due to the
> times of oppression and darkness and not knowing what
> tomorrow would bring that must have enhanced their actual
> relationship. I think that my father might have said: 'It's okay,
> you know, we love each other, so let's do what we can for
> today.' And that had it not been for the situation prevailing in
> 1936, then they would undoubtedly have got married.

Susi was at a loss as to how to begin the task of finding out about her father. So she did what had become second nature to her: she started firing off letters, to begin with to the tracing organizations she had contacted about her mother. Might the International Welfare Department of the British Red Cross have any information on Otto Hald? No, they did not. The German Embassy in London? The German Red Cross? Or its International Tracing Service in Arolsen? As one negative reply after another dropped through her letterbox, Susi realized that a completely different approach was called for. It was very unlikely she would make any progress based as she was in a small town in Warwickshire.

What she needed was an ally in the field, a Bertha Leverton figure, German-speaking of course, who would rally to her cause with the same degree of enthusiasm as the organizer of the Kindertransport reunion. But how to recruit such a friend?

Could there be any Halds in Munich? British Telecom's international directory enquiry service informed Susi that three Halds were currently listed in that city: Krystal, Nicholas and Brigitte. Instantly she plumped for the last, making a note of her telephone number and address. Never shy when it came to seeking information on her parents, Susi drafted a letter to Brigitte Hald that same evening.

Dear Mrs Hald

I obtained your name and address from International Tele-communication Services and am writing to ask your help in a personal matter. I wish to trace Mr Otto Hald, who will now be aged between 70 and 80 years. I know that he had a con-nection with Miss Rosa Bechhöfer in 1935/6, but have no other information. It would mean a great deal to me to be able to make contact with Mr Hald or any members of his family. I appreciate that you may be unable to help me with this request and, if not, would be grateful if you would give me the names and addresses of any other persons in Munich with the sur-name Hald.

I am not fluent in German and so am employing the services of a translation agency and shall be quite happy to do so in respect of any response. I can but thank you for any help you are able to give me in this matter and I wait to hear from you.

Yours sincerely

Grace Stocken

'I received a letter from England in the summer of 1988,' Brigitte Hald would later explain. 'It was from a Grace Stocken. It was translated into German as the writer could only speak English. She said she was looking for an Otto Hald. I had never heard of him. I'd never heard of the

Englishwoman either. Why was she looking for Otto Hald? I have to say that I was curious.'

So curious was Brigitte Hald that once Susi had told her the essential details of her story, she wrote to the public records office in Munich and began telephoning all the Halds whose numbers she could obtain. Had anyone heard of a rather elderly namesake called Otto? she asked.

Forty-three-old Brigitte, herself a twin, was a social worker whose parents had both been vociferous in their opposition to Nazism, although unlike many of those opposed to Hitler they had survived to tell their tale. Brigitte was to prove an effective ally – Susi did not know was that it was her way of attempting to make some good emerge from the enormous damage inflicted by the Nazis. 'I think I may have struck gold again,' Susi noted in her diary.

It was certainly not for want of trying, but after several months of probing and searching Brigitte was unable to report any progress at all. Some officials had been willing to co-operate; others had not. Sometimes records were available for public inspection, while in other cases it turned out that documents had been either lost or destroyed. Brigitte's phone bill grew rapidly, but not her file on Otto Hald. Nevertheless, every couple of months she would write to Susi to keep her fully informed – not that there was much to tell her. Thus, in the spring of 1989, she opened a letter which read: 'I write you again, although I don't have news at your father. I am so sorry.' In the summer there was still nothing to report. To Susi, grateful though she was, it was a depressingly familiar refrain.

Aware that Rosa and Otto's liaison had been illegal, Brigitte had even taken the trouble to write to those charged with keeping the documentation formerly held at Dachau, the concentration camp nearest to Munich. The first such camp, Dachau had claimed the lives of over 30,000 innocents, a considerable number of them the victims of bogus medical experiments. Perhaps, Brigitte thought, their relationship had attracted the attention of the Gestapo, for she was well aware that Jews and Gentiles caught together by chance – or more likely, informed on – had been rounded up and sent off to the camps. But she soon discovered that neither Rosa nor Otto was on any of the Dachau lists.

Despite the thoroughness of her research, and the considerable time, energy and money Brigitte continued to invest in her task, the only area in which there was any progress was in her relationship with Susi. The two women had soon forged a close, indeed intense, friendship. Therefore, although she had been unable to uncover any further information on Otto, Brigitte was pleased to write to Susi telling her how privileged she felt to be associated with her personally and with her quest. In fact, in under ten months she had come to embrace Susi's mission unreservedly, writing of the emotional bond she felt with her.

In Munich the search for Susi's father continued. Brigitte had continued to prod, pester and eventually propel the city's records office into action. At first its director, Hans Mühldorfer, had not been particularly helpful. But he had evidently come round to the view that there was only one way to free himself from Brigitte's incessant calls, and this was to make an effort and provide her with the material she required – not that he had been withholding it deliberately. It was just that such cases, where the facts were scarce, were notoriously difficult to pursue.

Nevertheless, on 24 August 1989 Herr Mühldorfer telephoned Brigitte, sounding unusually upbeat. Surely this time he had some good news for her. Indeed he did: he had managed to unearth Otto's birth certificate. Now he could disclose that Otto Hald had been born on 16 December 1907 in the little town of Göppingen, some twenty-five miles east of Stuttgart.

Immediately Brigitte launched a new line of enquiry. And this time, by contrast with her earlier frustrated efforts, within a few hours of receiving further details she had pieced together more of the Otto Hald jigsaw. She realized at once, however, that the picture which was emerging was unlikely to be attractive to anyone, least of all Susi, who had still to learn of this latest coup. However Brigitte reminded herself of her brief: it was not to censor or edit any information she might acquire, but to present it in its entirety. Later that evening she wrote to Susi, mindful of the delicacy her letter would require.

My dear Susi,

I have found your father's dates. Hans Mühldorfer telephoned me today. Otto Joseph Hald, born 16.12.07 in Göppingen. This town is in the German country [*Land*] of Baden-Württemberg. Otto left Munich in February 36, before your birth. Your poor mother! After the war he went to Leipzig and married there. He died here in West Germany aged about 60. He wasn't a good man, Gertrud May told me. I am sorry. All the Hald brothers are dead. I spoke to Gertrud today. She says that Otto was a man who liked women very much. But he didn't always tell the truth. He learned tinsmithing and finished his apprenticeship. He moved house frequently. Nobody knew of your existence.

Dear Susi, I am sure this information is not very pleasant for you. I am so sorry. We have an affinity and I am happy about this. We have found each other in the search for your father and I hope we can keep our friendship. I like you and look forward to our meeting one day. I am thinking of you and I wish to make good a little for all you have suffered.

With all my love,

Brigitte

For Susi confusion was the order of the day, as she rode high one moment only to plunge down low the next, borne along on an emotional roller-coaster. Buoyed up by learning of the existence of her father, she had learned simultaneously of his early death. It turned out that he had died in Marl on 5 August 1966. He was laid to rest at the age of fifty-eight, the years of heavy drinking having taken their toll.

So her father was dead. As for his life, it had hardly been a shining example of moral rectitude. Nobody denied the obvious fact that his behaviour had been disreputable, dishonest and cruel. Was he not guilty of the ultimate act of rejection, in abandoning twins before their birth and leaving their mother to fend for herself. As a pregnant but unmarried Jewess, Rosa Bechhöfer was doubly at risk in a society steeped in racial hatred and moral bigotry.

And yet for Susi, finding out about her father had been what she had set out to achieve. Now, thanks largely to the tireless work of Brigitte, she had been successful. As she wrote in her diary:

> I am so happy to know about this man, because life is all about KNOWING. Our fears come from the unknown. It was the not knowing that has always been the most difficult to endure, worse than anything I might ever find out. And yet, despite genuinely believing that as I sit here and write, recalling this journey of mine, there is a part of me that would, without any doubt, much rather have retained that wonderful fantasy of my father.

Susi had every reason to feel proud of herself, for her determination had led to the discovery of the truth. But it was not yet the whole truth.

EIGHT

Cousins Galore

As the reunion to mark the fiftieth anniversary of the Kindertransport approached, Bertha Leverton was working at a pace which alarmed her family and friends. She knew that without adequate publicity and promotion this key event, designed to highlight one of the Nazis' grossest sins, was likely to pass by unremarked. For Bertha, even to contemplate such a thing was itself a sin. It was imperative that she seize every opportunity to drive the message home. Therefore when visiting her sister in Israel it was only natural to Bertha to take advantage of her presence in that country by speaking on a radio programme to be broadcast by the English-language section of Kol Yisrael, part of the Israeli Broadcasting Authority. She pleaded with Efraim Geffen, the programme's producer, to allow her just thirty seconds at the end to mention one particular name. He agreed, and so listeners heard the message: 'Bertha Leverton has a special appeal regarding one of the former Kindertransport children', and then Bertha herself:

> Anybody who has heard of the name Bechhöfer – two little twins, and they were hardly three years old – and it was only recently that a surviving twin, now called Grace Stocken, who lives in a small town in England – she found out that her

name was Bechhöfer, that her father's name was Otto Hald
and her mother was called Rosa Bechhöfer from Munich. If
anybody has any recollection of someone called Bechhöfer,
would they please get in touch, because she is desperate to
find out who she was.

No sooner had the programme ended than listeners began to
phone in. It was as if, out of nowhere, an international Jewish
network had sprung into being, with names and telephone
numbers enthusiastically exchanged in a number of cities
around the world. The word soon spread to America, home
of six million Jews. A Mrs Orbach and a Mrs Bamberger
made contact to give the phone number of Mark Breuer,
both women stating that his sister Meta was married to Jerry
Bechhofer. This man, whose name apparently lacked the
umlaut, so that it was pronounced differently from Susi's,
was the head of a large family of orthodox Jews living in a
suburb of New York. Here, it seemed, was one possible
family member.

'When Bertha returned from Israel and told me that
people were coming forward, well, I went into ecstasies,'
recalls Susi. 'I said to myself: "Calm down, calm down now
– it might not be anybody." Alan told me to take it easy too
– because I would just go up to the ceiling. Of course it
might not be anybody, but then again, I thought, it could
equally be a big breakthrough.'

Before Susi was able to pursue this latest lead, Jerry
Bechhofer beat her to it.

October 17th, 1988

Dear Miss Bechhofer

One of your friends told us that you were on Kol Yisrael
News on October 7th and that you were looking for relatives.

If you are one of the daughters of Rosel Bechhofer, then
you are indeed my first cousin. My father was Bernhard
Bechhofer, one of Rosel's older brothers. Your mother, if she
was that, was the next-to-youngest sister of thirteen siblings.

Two brothers died young. Seven sisters perished in the Holocaust, one sister survived and died here app. 15 years ago. My father and his remaining two brothers died here – the last, Isaak – app. 12 years ago.

So, are you our cousin? If so, are you not one of twins?

Please write to us.

Sincerely

Jerry G. Bechhofer

'Well, yes, of course I'm one of the twins,' Susi exclaimed in her diary, 'so it's very clear to me not just that I'm Rosel's daughter, but that it is my first cousin writing to me.'

Barely a fortnight after his first, rather cautious enquiry, Jerry Bechhofer was back, this time outlining the history of the entire clan and enclosing a family tree. Now he too was in no doubt: a first cousin had indeed been found. 'Of course you are our cousin,' he wrote. 'It's very simple. Your mother was our Tante Rosel (we never called her Rosa), a very kind woman who did not have an easy life.'

Jerry went on to speak about Frieda, the eighth child of Gabriel and Sara Bechhöfer, Susi's and his mutual grand-parents. The only member of the family who had put herself out to help Rosa by covering her expenses during her pregnancy and then during her confinement, Frieda had died in a concentration camp. Three of Rosa's brothers had made it to America, but over half of the Bechhöfer children had perished in the gas chambers. The story of the Bechhöfers was, in this respect, that of the greater part of European Jewry in that dark time: they had been caught up in a programme of systematic slaughter the horror of which the world had not witnessed before or since. However, those who had survived had gone on to replenish the family stock, Jerry explained. On a more personal note, he said: 'I want to tell you how exciting and moving it is to have heard from you and to have "found" you. I hope that some day we meet in person. Ours is a very historic people and everyone counts

– very much. It's thrilling that now, instead of 8 cousins, we are 9.'

In fact, there were in the United States and elsewhere in the world cousins galore – at least two dozen second cousins and well over fifty second cousins once removed. Mainly orthodox Jews living strictly in accordance with the Torah, some members of the family had had six or seven children, others even more. Indeed, when Jerry had enclosed the family tree he had apologized because it was not quite up to date. 'For example, section II shows only 6 grandchildren for us. That was nine grandchildren ago. I hope all this is not too much family for you – after having been virtually without one all your life,' he added.

'Receiving this long letter was one of the most earth-shattering experiences of my life,' says Susi. The reasons were clear: at last someone had told her who her mother was, and that she had not just one but many living relatives. And then there was the shock of learning that many of my family had perished in the Holocaust. Up until now its horrors had been something that had happened to other people, and had in no way impinged on Susi's life. Making all these discoveries at once, she recalls, made her glimpse what it must be like to go crazy.

Bertha Leverton was thrilled for Susi and enormously gratified to have played a crucial role in reuniting her with her family. For had this not been her self-imposed brief from the start: to put the former children of the Kindertransport in touch with family, relatives and friends? Her objective achieved, Bertha did admit later: 'Sometimes I do feel a little guilty though, for having turned her life upside down.'

Not too guilty, however, to stop her dropping a strong hint to the *Jewish Chronicle*, the long-established newspaper of Britain's Jewry, that there was a story which could be of interest to them, namely the apparently successful outcome of Susi's search. Coverage of the story, Bertha was well aware, would also give welcome publicity to the Kindertransport reunion, now only a few months away.

A few days later Susi received a telephone call from Jenni Frazer, a journalist from the *Jewish Chronicle*. The newspaper, until that day unknown to Susi, did indeed want to run the story, regarding it as of enormous interest to the Jewish community.

'Refugee Susi Home At Last,' the paper announced, giving considerable prominence to the piece. 'Saved from the Nazis and raised as a Christian, Susi Bechhöfer has retraced her roots,' it added below. And there, surrounded by a moving account of Susi's quest to date, was a photograph of the twins at about four years of age, each child beautifully turned out in a pretty matching dress with a lace collar, and both smiling broadly.

The article was well written and caused something of a stir in Jewish circles, unaccustomed to tales with a happy ending. Nowhere was this more true than in the Bath home of an elderly lady by the name of Miss Edith Moses. She was not a regular subscriber to the *Jewish Chronicle*; it was by chance that she had bought that edition. She looked at the picture of the twins again and again, and became convinced that here were two little faces on which she had set eyes before.

'I shouted out to my sister: "I know those children",' she would later recount. I was very excited, very surprised. I said to my sister: "I must contact the JC straight away" – and that I was there at the home where they were.'

She was indeed. Edith Moses had been a teacher working at the Antonienheim in Munich from April 1938, a few weeks before the twins' second birthday. It was she who had seen Rosa Bechhöfer coming and going from the orphanage, always rushing, always looking fraught. Miss Moses herself had only just managed to escape from Germany in time.

If the breakthroughs were now coming thick and fast, this did not diminish the impact of every new discovery. In this

case Susi found it particularly distressing to learn of someone who not only knew her mother but who had witnessed
her pain at such close quarters.

"It is a very strange feeling,' Susi confided to her diary,
'as if the doors of the orphanage have been opened again.
Walking through its corridors again, and a return to being a
little girl. It's very confusing.'

> Edith remembers absolutely everything, even the gap in my
> teeth. She told me that we were put there when we were 6
> weeks old. I find this fact very difficult to look at. Not so
> much in terms of myself – but in terms of my mother –
> the pain that must have been hers. She gave a very graphic
> description of Rosa coming to the nursery, of seeing us both
> and having to leave us – and of how upset she used to be that
> she couldn't actually look after us. This is one of the hardest
> things of the whole picture to come to terms with.

Before long Susi and Edith Moses met. For the former
teacher the reunion was one of pure joy:

> It was simply wonderful to see Susi again. I stood here by the
> window and I waited for the taxi. I watched her get out of the
> taxi, went down the stairs and I said: 'My darling little Susi,
> did I ever think in my wildest dreams that I would ever see
> you again?' I just couldn't believe it – it was like a miracle.

For Susi it was also an unforgettable day, but because of the
feelings the meeting evoked, it was a bitter-sweet experience.
Back in Rugby that evening, Susi turned to her diary once
more. Only here, it seemed, could she express herself freely.

> The most significant day since May 18th 1939. 50 years ago I
> lost her and now have found this lovely lady. IF ONLY is what I
> came away with – if only the other plans she spoke of had
> come to fruition, then it would have been a home with a Jewish
> family in California. Or at least a home in the orphanage
> knowing my mother – if only there hadn't been a war. But no –

it was a childhood of misery. At least now though there is a future that holds the promise of recapturing some of the things that were lost – my name, my Jewish heritage and family.

Quite unconsciously, Susi had developed a strategy for survival. She would simply switch off at various points, anaesthetizing herself against the pain, despite the clear therapeutic value of her diary. For she could only absorb so much information at any one time. So whenever the occurrence of the name Rosa Bechhöfer seemed to threaten great pain, Susi simply refused to confront the situation directly. She would distract or distance herself from any information which she felt to be unappealing, unfavourable, or in any way damaging to her cause. For ever since Jerry Bechhofer had started to correspond with the new cousin whom he had yet to meet, he did not disguise his view that Rosa was most unlikely to have survived the war. Was Susi therefore not clinging to false hopes?

'It seems strange to me that she should have made her way to England in 42 or 43,' he wrote. 'The Germans didn't let anyone out any more at that time. Where is your information that she came to England?'

In answering this question Susi was pleased to be able to refer to the documents she had received from the Central British Fund, and indeed to that organization's covering letter, in which the secretary had categorically stated that Rosa Bechhöfer had come to England to work as a domestic servant in April 1943. Susi sent photocopies of the material, hoping her cousin might come to share her belief that Rosa might still be alive. But Jerry Bechhofer, always meticulous when it came to chronicling his family's history, was not impressed.

'What is the C.B.F.?' he asked in a subsequent exchange of letters. 'It occurs to me that perhaps this was just an application from her to come to the U.K. Or do you have knowledge that she actually came to England? If she did then it should be possible to trace her. In those days one had to register, even if one was an alien.'

Another cousin, Senta, the daughter of Susi's newly acquired aunt, the sprightly 94-year-old Martha, likewise made contact to suggest that Rosa was no longer alive, contending that she had had breast cancer at some unspecified date, after which she had been deported to a camp.

'Impossible,' Susi wrote in her diary. 'I say NO. I can't bear this thought; this has to be the worst scenario. I will prove otherwise.'

If Susi was stubbornly refusing to countenance the idea that her mother had perished along with a number of other Bechhöfers, so was her son, although their perspectives differed. Now busy working for his final examinations at St Catherine's College, Cambridge, Frederick had from the outset displayed little enthusiasm for the venture. What good could possibly come of it, he wondered. 'If my grandmother went to a concentration camp,' he declared, 'then that is something that I just don't want to know.'

The organ scholar was equally dismissive when Jerry pointed out in one of his letters that in the eyes of Jewish law Frederick was a Jew himself, born as he was of a Jewish mother. 'Well, he would say that, wouldn't he?' was his initial response. Yet, despite his repeated protestations to the contrary, Frederick would in time develop a keen interest in the issues raised by his mother's search for her roots.

On 18 May 1989, fifty years to the day since the twins had arrived in England, Susi flew to New York's John F. Kennedy Airport to meet the American Bechhofers for the first time. Before she left, Alan had continued to play the role of devil's advocate, warning his wife: 'You don't know what these people are like. You don't know what their customs and beliefs are going to be.' Not that it mattered to Susi, because whatever their religious practices or idiosyncrasies, they were her family now.

Although she was nervous about flying, Susi dismissed from her mind the idea that the plane might crash, telling herself over and over that her mission was too important for that to happen. Deprived of any blood ties since the death of Eunice, she had often fantasized about what long-lost relatives she might have, and now the moment was at hand when she would see her family face to face.

Relatives! The very word was music to her ears. Even so, after an eight-hour flight and a long delay in Immigration, she was more than a little keyed up as she hurried to meet the welcoming party at John F. Kennedy Airport. She had had scarcely any contact with the relatively assimilated Jews of England, let alone a group of fundamentalist orthodox Jews from New York. Unsurprisingly, they displayed none of the British reserve that she was so used to.

The first thing she saw was the big banner they had made. 'WELCOME SUSI,' it said, putting her at ease right away. Today she recalls that she had in her mind the idea that, because of their strict religion, the men might shun physical contact and, strangely, she cannot remember whether they touched her or not. Whatever the truth, as her new family introduced themselves one by one, the warmth of their words and their smiles touched her feelings deeply. 'They all wanted to know everything at once, and bombarded me with questions unanswered for fifty years, even though I was dog-tired from the journey,' Susi remembers. 'Understandably, they were just as curious about me as I was about them.'

In a complete whirl, Susi was whisked off to her cousin Senta's apartment in the suburb of Kew Gardens, where the whole clan was to enjoy a kosher meal together in Susi's honour. Orthodox-Jewish life was completely unfamiliar to Susi, and among the many questions in her mind was why they were eating off paper plates and using plastic cutlery.

The simple answer was that the Kashrut, the Jewish dietary laws, demanded it.

The family talked well into the night, and partly because she was exhausted and partly because they were so many of them, she put aside for the moment the questions she wanted to ask and instead tried to answer theirs. How had her quest to find her mother's family begun? they wanted to know. What did it feel like to have no blood relatives? Why had it all taken so long?

Susi's upbringing and expectations of family life could hardly have been more different, and yet she could see that here was a real family: interdependent, trusting and secure. For a while her thoughts grew sad as she asked herself where all the years had gone, and reflected on how much of her life had gone by without knowing these fine people, many of whom, like her, were now greying and middle-aged.

The life of the Bechhofers could hardly have been more different from the cold, severe world of Welsh Baptist non-conformism in which Susi had spent her childhood. Judaism was the driving force of their lives. In fact, the Bechhofers remain followers of a particular form of orthodox Judaism. Unlike the Jews of the Reform movement, who believe that Judaism ought to be tailored to meet the requirements of modern life, dispensing with various inconvenient rituals in the process, the Bechhofers maintain that the law should be adhered to, since it was given by God on Mount Sinai. In particular they are ardent followers of Rabbi Samson Raphael Hirsch, the father of modern orthodoxy, and each one of them practises the principle of Torah im Derech Eretz: living by all the commandments of the Torah, albeit within the context of the modern world. Hirsch, long recognized as one of the great Jewish thinkers, had developed the system of Neo-Orthodoxy, a theology which had helped to make orthodox Judaism flourish in Germany in the nineteenth century.

Jerry Bechhofer was very proud of the fact that his late father-in-law was the grandson of the sainted Rabbi himself. Jerry's father-in-law, Rabbi Dr Joseph Breuer, had not only lived to the age of ninety-eight, but had also founded a school shortly before the end of the Second World War: the Yeshiva Rabbi Samson Raphael Hirsch. It was to this school that the Bechhofers devoted the greater part of their time, energy and love.

Among the enduring relationships that Susi was to forge on that trip was one with Sonya Loeb, Jerry's sister and so also a first cousin. Like her brother, she had been most warm and welcoming from the moment they had first met. 'And don't you ever think,' Sonya had commanded in a letter to Susi before her visit, 'as you sometimes indicate in your letters, that we will ever tire of you, or of your being with us. We will not.'

Everything that Susi did with the Bechhofers was to bear out the truth of that promise. Sonya and Senta had arranged a busy schedule for her. This came as no surprise, for again and again one relative or another had said how much time they had to make up after all the lost years. Among other engagements, Susi accompanied Senta to several fund-raising luncheons for Hadassah, a charity that lends financial support to hospitals in Israel. It was on such an occasion that she heard the Israeli national anthem for the first time, and was moved by the selfless dedication to their cause of this group of elegant and capable women.

There followed a visit to the Jewish Museum and, with each day seemingly hotter than the last, exhausting trips to see the sights of New York. Maceys, Bloomingdales and Manhattan's other big stores were also on the itinerary, as was an attractive shopping mall in New Jersey, the like of which Susi had never seen before. When it came to eating in restaurants with her hosts, Susi was struck by the fact, for all the city's amazing culinary choice, there were very few available to them, since they could eat only in strictly kosher establishments approved by Beth Din.

On bank holiday Monday cousin Ernie and his wife Edna gave a barbecue so that everyone could meet Susi, either again or for the first time. Susi talked with Leo, who had been in the concentration camps and whose mother, Sophie, had perished there. She found it difficult to imagine what Leo must feel on looking back, and wondered if she, with her story of flight from Germany, was a painful reminder of that nightmare. Yet in the end she could only marvel at how well adjusted, indeed relaxed, he seemed. Nor was he the only one to have assimilated the past so honestly and to live so fully in the present.

To Susi, the pace, the sights and the sounds of that huge city were at first quite alien. At times she longed for the safety and peace of home, for the familiarity of St Andrew's Parish Church in Rugby, where throughout her quest she had continued to play the organ and sing hymns, together with Hazel Bell and a small group of friends. And yet she had wanted earnestly to find her family, sometimes with an all-consuming force. And here, in suburban New York, was where they happened to be.

While doing her best to acquaint herself with and respect the many laws of the Torah, she nevertheless slipped up more than once, carrying a spectacle case here, ringing a door bell there. Such acts are among those forbidden on the Sabbath, although these minor transgressions did not irk the Bechhofers in the slightest, merely bringing wry smiles to their faces. For they knew very well that they could hardly expect Susi suddenly to conduct herself like an orthodox Jewess.

'They are all lovely,' Susi recorded in her diary while in New York, 'but I still can't help feeling like a fish out of water.' Here is my family, part of her felt, and this is where I belong, but another voice inside her said that she most certainly did not. How could she, with fifty years of English Christianity instilled into her, feel at home in what she saw as a 'ghetto of orthodoxy'? One thing was clear: she needed time and space to sort out her true feelings.

Jerry was particularly sensitive to his cousin's plight. The existence of cultural and religious differences between them had not prevented intense feelings from surfacing, right from the outset. Even before Susi's arrival, Jerry had not hesitated to express his joy at learning of her existence. 'We, the family, have talked much about what it must have been like for you before you were married,' he had written, 'to be literally *alone in the world* and now to find that there are people who are your own flesh and blood and who love you. Surely no one else who has not been in a similar position can properly feel how this must be.'

It was while in New York that Susi Stocken metamorphosed into Susi Bechhöfer. And a Susi Bechhöfer who could point to a large and loving family. This was for her the most exciting aspect of the whole trip. After so many long and lonely years, it was as if a gloriously bright light had been switched on. Now, after nearly half a century, the little German Jewish girl who had been left to fend for herself in Munich's Jewish orphanage, had been resurrected. And there were more miracles: not only had she been brought back to life again, but she was now an altogether more cheerful and better-balanced person, far more at ease with herself than Grace had ever been.

There was one other revolution in her life too. Susi had finally become a daughter: the daughter of Rosa Bechhöfer. For again and again she found herself being addressed as such, her mother being likewise referred to by name. How different from the days of her childhood: no more dark secrets now. Now she could ask about her mother as much as she liked – and she did. Kind-hearted, happy, stylish – she loved and knew how to use colours – were some of the descriptions of Rosa she was given. 'You look just like your mother,' was something she heard again and again – from Jerry, Aunt Martha and everyone else old enough to cast their mind back half a century. 'She had such beautiful hands. I notice yours are not the same!' said someone with the characteristic candour of New York's Jews.

Rosa seemed to live among them as they evoked her presence, and Susi seized the opportunity to be her daughter to the full, for the simple reason that she had never received her fair share of mothering. True, she had had a foster mother. But Irene Mann's energies had been expended almost exclusively on Eunice, especially – and understandably – during the long years of her illness. In addition, the Reverend Mann had always made it quite clear that he wished to play the central role in Susi's life. And his theory had been put into practice to the letter, for he had seen to it that all others were excluded, including his wife. He had his own reasons for wishing to feature so prominently in his daughter's life. But whatever his motives – sexual, psychological or otherwise – the result was that there had been very little space in which Irene had been able, or indeed allowed, to operate as a mother. Therefore to become Rosa's daughter once more tasted particularly sweet, even though so many years had passed since Susi had lain in her mother's arms as a baby.

A remarkable family reunion was taking place. 'I had had this name Bechhöfer in the back of my mind for all these years,' Susi said at the time, 'and now finally I have met up with my family. They thought I had perished in the Holocaust. But here I am. It's like a fairy tale come true.'

There was no denying the fact that Rosa Bechhöfer's life had been anything but a fairy tale. However, when the question of her attempts to reach her family in the United States came up, Susi remained characteristically pragmatic. All that, she told herself, belonged to the past, and she was not interested in voicing recriminations against anybody, least of all elderly relatives who had themselves been damaged by Hitler's regime.

Before Susi had gone to America, she had received a remarkable gift from her new family. 'When I saw these photographs of my mother I was quite simply elated,' she explains. 'I had always thought that if I could just have one photograph, then my life would feel totally different. Yet at the same time I could hardly bear to look at them.'

Her heart thumping and her hands trembling, Susi forced herself to concentrate on the image she had so long wanted to see. As she looked into that face memories began to stir in her – the pallor of her mother's skin, her straight black hair, most often scraped back in a bun, and the laughter that was hidden deep in her tired eyes. And then, bizarrely, came a flood of recollections of Miss Bennett, her headmistress all those years ago. Susi saw in an instant why she had felt such a fierce love for her; why, even at the risk of angering her, she had tried ceaselessly to win her attention.

Unaware at the time of what she was doing, she had sought the love her mother might have supplied. In her mind the images of her mother and Miss Bennett had long been merged. Now, holding in her hand the means to separate them, she understood so much about her childhood behaviour and the longing for a mother's love that had been with her throughout her life. It was too late to possess the love of the woman whose face she saw before her, but now she had something at least as precious: she had a focus for the daughterly love she wanted to express. She began to understand that to give is indeed a greater thing than to receive. And, in finding her mother and her long-buried feelings towards her, she was beginning to find herself.

Aunt Martha understood very well the significance of the pictures. 'If I had not kept these photos, Susi would not have any,' she said when Susi visited her and her daughter

Senta one day at her apartment. 'I'm not superstitious, but I do think it was meant that I kept the photos. It was inspired by God. I have lived a long life – long enough to hand over the photos. Isn't that a miracle? Thank God for this.'

Back in Rugby, scarcely accustomed to being home after a flood of new experiences in America, Susi headed for a shop where she was now a well-known customer: the picture framer's. As well as the photographs of Rosa, which were now her most precious possessions, she had some prints of members of the family from the last century which had been given to her by the Bechhofers. Before long these photographs were on display in Susi's living room.

Pleased though he was that Susi had discovered relatives she never knew she had, Alan could not see the point of making the home a shrine to these gloomy images of the past. It was all rather overpowering, coming into the room and being confronted by a gallery of strange men in flat hats, long coats and big, bushy beards. He began to feel crowded out of his own home, and made no bones about it.

Awaiting Susi on her return was a letter from the Home Office. It was in reply to her earlier request for details of her mother's date of entry into Britain. The reply was bitterly disappointing: there was still no trace of Rosa whatsoever. Susi's diary reads:

> I am beginning to wonder if she did come to this country after all. Perhaps the CBF document was just a registration number sent by post, as Jerry suggested in his letter. I have reached a blind alley in my search. But I must persevere, turn every stone until I find out what did happen to Rosa. This is the single most important aspect of the whole search.

And persevere she did, for she promptly drafted an advertisement and then forwarded it to the CBF for inclusion in its magazine, read by thousands of Jewish former refugees.

Persisting, despite all the evidence to the contrary, in the belief that Rosa had indeed reached England, she made a simple plea that concealed a lifetime of longing:

INFORMATION REQUIRED

ROSA BECHHOFER. BORN 7.7.1898. REGISTERED AS
A DOMESTIC SERVANT 30.4.1943. MOTHER OF TWINS.
ANYBODY WHO REMEMBERS HER PLEASE CONTACT
BOX NUMBER 82. URGENT.

NINE
Martina

'Susi. You've got a sister!' It was Brigitte Hald calling from Munich. Not content with having unearthed Otto's birth certificate and several other important facts about Susi's father, the indefatigable social worker turned researcher had produced a real gem this time. Brigitte had spent nearly a year engaged in fruitless and often frustrating detective work – and then, finally, success. Having come to identify so closely with Susi's goal, she knew as she dialled her number that the news would thrill her friend, and she was proud to be the bearer.

Brigitte hurried through the sequence of events which had led her to learn of this new addition to Susi's family. The key to it all, she explained, had been obtaining the copy of Otto's birth certificate, for this had provided her with a geographical framework within which to concentrate her efforts. From that moment onwards there had followed one lead after another. She had discovered that, long before the eventual collapse of Otto and Luisa's marriage – within six months of their wedding, in fact – Luisa had given birth to a daughter. Susi spotted at once that here was history repeating itself: the child had been conceived out of wedlock, as Susi and Lotte had been before her. But there the similarity ended, for whereas Otto had deserted Rosa on learning of her plight, he had married the pregnant Luisa.

Susi's half-sister turned out to be Martina Uhlitzsch, a 46-year-old married woman born and still living in Leipzig, the second largest city in East Germany. The shock had been even greater for Martina, for it was not she who had dispatched search parties in an attempt to find long-lost relatives. She had always been well aware of the circumstances of her upbringing, indeed unhappily so. Her role in the discovery that Brigitte had made was simply to have been there, and to have displayed, after initial reservations, a willingness to help:

> One evening in October 1989 I had a phone call from a Brigitte Hald. She asked if Otto Hald was my father. 'Yes,' I said, 'that's right. He was born on 16 December 1907.' She said: 'You'd better sit down!' Brigitte then explained everything to me. To begin with I thought that perhaps she was having me on, because I do tend to be a bit suspicious. But anyway I rang her back, because nobody could have known that my father was Otto Hald. That was impossible. The story just had to be true.

Just as when she had learned of the existence of the American Bechhofers, Susi was not at all sure what to do with this startling discovery. Alone at home, she had no one at that moment with whom to share it, not even her husband. But then, she had often mused, was there anyone, apart from Bertha and Brigitte, who was truly interested in the outcome of her search? By now used to dealing with these things alone, she quietly thanked Brigitte and, images of Bechhöfers and Halds flitting through her mind, sat down with a cup of tea to watch the early-evening news on the television.

Calm she might have felt, but what she saw on the screen soon changed that. The main story concerned the massive demonstrations in Leipzig, where communism was in its death throes, as indeed it soon would be throughout the German Democratic Republic. Susi recalls:

I just couldn't believe it. To begin with, I didn't even know exactly where Leipzig was. Was it East, West, North, or South Germany? And there on my telly I am suddenly looking at pictures of Leipzig, and I've just been told that I have got a sister there. There – is she out there demonstrating with the crowds, I wonder?

It was not long before the telephone rang again in Martina's home in Mozartstrasse. This time it was Susi calling. Despite the fact that her knowledge of German had long gone and Martina knew not a word of English, their first brief exchange said all that needed to be said for the moment:

'Susi.'
  'Martina.'
  'Schwester.'
  'Sister.'

Susi remembers: 'After those few words we really weren't talking any language at all. We were just umming and aahing. And we know that we are sisters. We were both thrilled. It was a tremendous moment for the two of us. Even though we couldn't really talk to one another, we both knew exactly what was going on.'

At her end of the line Martina was in tears, as was her husband, Detlef. She might not have instigated the search, but she was just as exhilarated as Susi to have found so close a blood link to her father. Ever since the death of her mother Luisa, nine years earlier, Martina had also found herself stripped of all family. Nor had she ever tried to disguise the greatest source of sadness in her life: the inability to have a child of her own. Only a very happy marriage to a caring and supportive man had helped to ward off an ever-present undercurrent of loneliness.

Susi and Martina began to correspond, with Brigitte translating both women's letters for them. To begin with, Martina spoke highly of their father. He had always been full of life, she explained chirpily, and was the very greatest of fun to be with when she was a child. Not only that: he was also a colourful and creative personality with enormous enthusiasm for so many aspects of life. However, as a trust began to develop between the sisters, Martina became less protective of Otto. Slowly the truth began to emerge.

Her father had caused her a great deal of pain. After separating from Luisa he often insisted on taking her with him on jaunts to see various girlfriends. Forty years later, Martina still found the experience painful to talk about. Otto also sent her repeatedly to convey the same message to his estranged wife: In future there will be no more women and no more wine. For Luisa, her husband's legendary charm had long since worn thin, and she would have none of his efforts to tug at her heartstrings by using their daughter as a go-between.

And then came Martina's most grievous wound. Her beloved father – for that he had remained, regardless of his inadequacies – mysteriously disappeared with his house-keeper, never to return. Martina was just eleven at the time. It was similar to the brutal way in which he had treated Susi's mother eighteen years earlier. At least then, had he sunk to it, he could have cited the Nuremberg Laws, claiming in his defence that theirs was a proscribed relationship so that it was best for both of them that it should end. But now, under no legal threat, he could not find it in himself to say goodbye to his own daughter, preferring to slip away into the night.

Nor did Otto's hurried departure mark the end of Martina's suffering at his hands. For she witnessed her mother's anguish too, much of which was financial rather than emotional in origin. Despite her subsequent divorce from Otto, Luisa remained liable for his sizeable debts, largely unpaid tax on income from sales of his welding products in East Germany. The settlement was scarcely equitable: a deserted wife obliged to settle her ex-husband's debts while he paid nothing what-soever in maintenance.

In the face of these formidable odds Luisa pushed herself hard. She was determined to make up for the absence of a father figure in Martina's life. Whenever she could, she would put in overtime at work so as to be able to take her daughter to concerts, and did her utmost to encourage her obvious penchant for music and the arts. With its strong musical traditions, Leipzig was an ideal place in which to live, and Martina often heard the city's celebrated Gewandhaus Orchestra and Thomaner Choir, and later on was a frequent visitor to the handsome new opera house.

Yet for young Martina the finest music in the land could never compensate for the loss of the man she had adored, and throughout her teens she often wondered if she had in some way been responsible for his flight. She pondered too how different her life might have been if she had been more effective as a go-between. Inwardly she would rebuke herself for not having tried harder. Throughout her adolescence, and indeed beyond, hardly a day went by in which she did not think of her father: her every thought about him a potent cocktail of love, anger and sadness.

Amid all Martina's revelations about their father's behaviour was something else that had an equally profound effect on Susi. One of Martina's letters to Susi contained a photograph of Otto. For the first time Susi could see what her father looked like. But it was not his face or build that most struck her when she first set eyes on the ageing print. The photograph showed a German soldier kitted out in a standard-issue greatcoat, a rifle slung over his right shoulder, and, sitting squarely on his head, the all too familiar steel helmet of the war years. This was Otto Hald, her father. But was he not also the enemy?

'When I saw that photograph,' Susi recalls, 'I was really quite shattered.'

When you embark upon a project like this, you have to be
prepared for absolutely anything. And really in a way this is
the scenario that I didn't want to see. But at the same time
he's my father there, standing in his German uniform. In my
fantasy I had wanted him to be this dashing man, who was
perhaps somebody I could have loved. I'm not saying that I
can't love him. Just that I obviously can't love what he is
standing there representing – the enemy.

Then a series of photographs of Otto began to arrive from
Martina via Brigitte. Having been deprived of any information about her roots all through her life, Susi felt the need
to surround herself with these images of the father she had
never known. Her husband was far from pleased. 'It was all
very well for her,' he insists, 'but I could hardly understand
how she would want to exhibit all of those photographs
around the house when he had caused such an upheaval.
Otto looks rather miserable to me.... He was also rather
naughty in my view – a ladies' man through and through.'
Susi stands by her decision:

In fact, I put those photographs of Otto up because a lot of
the information about my father has been very distressing for
me. I just find that out of the two father figures in my life –
well, I wouldn't have chosen either of them. I feel as if I have
been abused by them both, although in different ways of
course. So surrounding myself with his photographs was a way
of trying to come to terms with some sort of father figure. So
there was a method in my madness.

But her plan was not entirely successful, because with the
passage of time the appeal of Otto's portraits began to fade,
just like the black and white images themselves. Susi came
to realize that the rather doleful figure staring at her from
the living-room mantelpiece and elsewhere in the house
simply represented pain for everyone concerned. Rosa
Bechhöfer had suffered at his hands. Susi and Lotte had too.

Eventually all the photographs were consigned to the loft, Alan breathing a sigh of relief as he stored them away.

In the meantime Susi had come to accept her father as he was, aware of the fact that she had 'let Otto off the hook'.

> I don't know why, but I do. I choose to attribute a lot of his 'bad behaviour' more to the times than to my father as such, because Otto was Aryan and Rosa was Jewish – and he must surely have been left with no alternative other than to leave her. I just can't bring myself to view him as being all tied up with the Nazis and Nazism. I say that just because Otto was *the* enemy that doesn't make him *my* enemy. What I do realize, though, is that a considerable chunk of the fantasy which I had about my father – as a dashing and debonair young officer who had loved and struggled hard to be with my mother – was, to quite a large degree, hogwash. So that has been rather painful for me to look at too.

Sally George, the TV producer, was aware of the dramatic progress Susi had been making in her search for her roots. During that time they had often discussed the idea of a documentary about Susi. Sally had ruled out the idea of her featuring in the programme on the Kindertransport children, for the good reason that Susi could not remember what had happened to her, whereas she needed subjects who could. In the light of Sally's decision, and knowing how complex a business it was to make a television film, Susi had taken a phlegmatic view of her story's chances of ever reaching the screen. Nor did she imagine that the discovery of a half-sister in Leipzig would change matters much.

But when Susi told her the news Sally saw at once that here was too good an opportunity to miss. She resolved instantly to do her best to be there with a film crew to record Susi and Martina's first meeting. Aware that she must act rapidly, within weeks she had won the necessary consents for a programme to be made. After eighteen months of stop–

start discussions and delays, the filming of 'Whatever Happened to Susi?' could at last get under way.

In anticipation of the journey, Susi wrote in her diary:

> Back to Munich after 50 years. It is the right time. Here I will absorb my past left behind and integrate it with the present. I believe that Martina is the gift that will replace my father's absence. I thank God for the many many people who are enabling me to make this unique journey.

It was Brigitte Hald who, efficient as ever, had arranged for the sisters to meet in Munich, the collapse of communism now enabling her to travel freely to the West. As Susi waited on the platform at the city's main station, Martina's train was fast approaching the Bavarian capital, having travelled south from Leipzig through an East Germany in transition, before crossing the Danube and entering the last stage of the journey. Although they had exchanged many letters and photographs, both women wondered, with a mixture of apprehension and excitement, what it would be like to actually see and hold each other for the first time.

At last the train pulled in and there was Martina. Beside her was Detlef, Teddy as she called him, who had no intention of missing the big moment. Susi recalls:

> And then I saw her. Well, you just want to hold one another and say: 'This is it. We are sisters. We have the same father.' And I can actually acknowledge for the first time that I had a father. That might seem a strange thing for someone in their fifties to say, but that was the truth of it. I was actually able to acknowledge that here was something real of my father – in the form of Martina. So everything inside just opened up and I guess I felt feelings that I've not experienced before. That was quite frightening in a way. But I'm sure that Martina felt the same way. I hadn't bargained for such an emotional moment at all.

There was another reason for the tears that suddenly overwhelmed Susi. For as she looked at her half-sister in the flesh for the first time, she noticed at once the startling resemblance between Martina and her late twin. It was not just the colour of the eyes and the style of the hair, but many other details too – right down to the square, gold-rimmed glasses. In fact, the likeness was a little eerie, for Lotte – Susi had reverted to using Eunice's original name – had been laid to rest nearly twenty years earlier.

The feeling that she was greeting Lotte made Susi feel rather uncomfortable. She had blocked out all thoughts of her twin in order to survive; suddenly, on seeing Martina, all of those memories came rushing back and she was not at all sure she wanted them. She realizes now that the pain was because she had never properly examined the total loss of Lotte. How bizarre that here, standing before Susi all these years later, should be a Lotte Bechhöfer–Eunice Mann incarnate. Martina's hug was heartfelt and straightforward, but for Susi there was another level of complexity. How could she embrace Martina unreservedly when she had still to embark on the process of mourning the premature loss of her sister?

The intensity of the moment began to fade, and Susi and Martina left for Brigitte's flat, where they would spend some quieter, less dramatic time together. With Brigitte acting as interpreter, they exchanged gifts and yet more photographs, one of which in particular caught Susi's attention. It was a black and white print of Otto holding Martina's hand when she was about eight. 'Somehow I slotted myself in there, into that photograph,' Susi explained later. 'And in my imagination my father is holding my hand. I just kept thinking to myself: my hand should be there too. Why had he never been there for me?'

Susi knew already of the pain Otto had brought Martina, but now she discovered that the photograph showed one of the rare occasions when their hands had been intertwined. As the sisters reminisced, they realized how strange it was that, as a result of the most haphazard of quests, they should find themselves together, two innocent victims of the same man's neglect and selfishness.

Although communication between them was restricted by language difficulties, no words were called for when Martina presented to Susi a gift which could not have been more personal or precious. It was their father Otto's ring, which he had given to Martina when she was just three years of age. While it clearly pained her to part with it, since it was one of the few possessions which evoked the all too short time they had spent together, Martina nevertheless felt great pleasure in passing it on to her new-found sister, who had never once found herself in that same father's arms. It was Martina's way of apologizing on Otto's behalf for his appalling treatment of Susi, Lotte and their mother. Yet, to some extent still protective of her father, Martina remains reluctant to condemn him, and on this the half-sisters continue to agree.

Martha Bechhofer also happened to choose the same token with which to express her love and concern for her long-lost niece. She also gave Susi a ring, one which had belonged to Rosa. Susi now wears both rings with pride, although there are times when she looks down at them and does not know whether to laugh or cry.

> There's just so much irony about it all. The laughter is my
> saying to myself: 'Little did you think when you acquired
> these rings that one day Susi, the little girl from the orphan-
> age, would be wearing them.' And the crying is about my
> acknowledging that whilst I have finally succeeded in getting
> Otto and Rosa together in symbolic fashion on my finger,
> neither parent was available for me as a child and beyond.

All too soon it was time for Martina and Detlef to leave. Although it had been a day she would never forget, Martina was anxious to return to her administrative job in Leipzig.

For over thirty years she had held down a position of some responsibility. But now, she explained, despite her loyalty and long service, the demands of East Germany's fledgling market economy meant that the notion of a secure job was already a quaint one.

A few days later, with the help of Brigitte, she wrote to Susi, as ever finding it much easier to express herself on paper than in person.

My dear Susi

Teddy and I want to tell you that we are very happy to find you. We are glad that we have seen you for the first time. Often we think at the times in München. I wish to thank you for the common hours with you as I could hold your hand and see into your lovely eyes.

We are living now in a new country and we have to assimilate to it. Yes, I am anxious for my beautiful job. I cannot say with words how much I wish to thank you for the wonderful presents. Why have you given so much money for us? Your presence was gift enough.

To you, my dear sister, all my love and God's blessing.

Your loving sister

Martina

When it came to replying, there was only one thought in Susi's mind; only one that seemed to matter. After so many years of being alone, and of being unaware of her own identity, she had at last found her father's family. She knew she could hardly have got closer to Otto Hald than that. It had unearthed all manner of strange feelings, many of them bound up with the past. Yet Susi was in no doubt that every moment had been worthwhile, even those that had at first troubled her. For in experiencing and sharing new emotions she had got to know the sister she had just found.

'We are sisters,' she proclaimed to Martina, 'and no one can ever take that away from us.'

For the BBC unit filming went smoothly enough, but Sally George knew that in order to complete Susi's story it was essential to find out what had become of Rosa. Unbeknown to Susi, she assigned a small team of researchers to this key question, instructing them to carry on from the point Susi and Bertha had reached. Having already made a film about the broader issue of the Kindertransport, Sally, like Jerry Bechhofer, had her doubts as to whether Rosa ever found her way to England. And yet she knew that speculation alone was not enough.

Now she too was committed to finding out the truth about Rosa.

TEN

Passport to Destruction

‘I don't want to be unkind to Grace,' insisted the Reverend Mann, feigning generosity and hurt in equal measure,

but we do feel that what we have done has been thrown back at us because she has shut us out of her life and grown apart from us over the years. Both my wife and I have had our moments when we thought that it might perhaps have been better to have followed the advice of the German Jewish Aid Committee after all – which was to have separated the twins upon their arrival in London. Whereupon we suddenly swallow our words and say how wrong that would have been. And we rebuke ourselves for even having had the thought at all.

For her part, Susi, having shown a reluctance to confront her adoptive father over the abuse which had dominated her later childhood and teenage years, had decided as an adult that the most satisfactory solution was to distance herself from Edward Mann. In the event, it was only after marrying Alan Stocken that she really felt free to do this, and even then her relationship with her father was not to be redefined as easily as she had hoped.

From the start Susi resolved that if independence had been hard won she would defend it just as vigorously. Nevertheless she decided not to challenge or confront the

Reverend, now in retirement, in any way. The approach she adopted was to be the hallmark of their relationship for many years: she simply ignored him. He was to be dealt with at arm's length, and allowed only the most grudging involvement in her or her family's life.

In fact at one time Susi did try another approach to exorcizing the pain of her bizarre relationship with her adoptive father. In October 1988, while she was searching for her real father, she sought the assistance of a therapist. She knew that she still had to confront the destructive influence of her powerful and manipulative adoptive father, who had been such a dominant force during her formative years and beyond.

Aware that her client was rather talented with her pen, the therapist suggested that Susi should try to write about any negative feelings that were troubling her. At first Susi found this difficult, but soon the words were flowing freely, even incoherently, so powerful were the feelings she had dammed up.

19.10.88

I was asked to express how I feel about you E.J. Mann – you were given a gift – a child to love – what you did was DESTROY – I FEEL DEEP BITTERNESS, RESENTMENT AND ANGER – the latter I am scared of. It might ERUPT and destroy all I have bravely fought to build. And so I bury this emotion knowing that as I do this I am partly immobilized.

How did you DESTROY me? You abused me mentally and physically. A LEECH sucking my life blood. You chained my whole being. You are a DIRTY UNCLEAN HYPOCRITE PREACHING TO OTHERS – abusing me by ACTS OF CRUELTY.

How were these MANIFESTED? I will tell you – you bastard. You would creep into my bed at 10 yrs and insert your filthy p into my v. I WOULD HAVE FEELINGS OF HATE FOR YOU, but also FEELINGS OF INSECURITY LEST I DENY you what you wanted under the pseudo-excuse of THIS ACT MAKING ME YOUR FLESH AND BLOOD. YOU ARE SICK – YOU WOULD MAKE

ME HOLD YOUR FILTHY P FOR A THRILL I GUESS and as I developed you would the life blood from me denying me rightful relationships. WHY? I guess you were SCARED I would talk. I didn't then but I will NOW. I WOULD LIKE TO SAY 'MAY YOU ROT IN HELL' BUT NO, I CAN'T LIVE WITH SUCH DESTRUCTION. YOU MUST PAY THE PRICE AS 'GOD' CHOOSES. FIRST THOUGH THERE IS DEBRIS TO THROW AWAY. I MUST FREE MYSELF FROM YOUR BONDAGE – YOU ARE A SNAKE ENCROACHING me with your sting.

While the Reverend Mann never saw this expression of his foster daughter's pent-up rage, her coldness towards him was unmistakable. And even though his complaints about being excluded revealed a certain disingenuousness, since the reasons for her contempt were obvious; they were not groundless. The truth was that, unhappy unless exercising complete control, he was furious.

In one particularly forceful letter in an acrimonious correspondence that spanned several years he warned Susi that, unless she abandoned her frosty stance and started to be a proper daughter to him once more, he would have to curtail her visits. He also made it clear that he was not willing to be fobbed off with either Alan or Frederick as surrogates for her. His ultimatum was that unless he and his wife could see Susi alone, whether at the Manns' home or hers, there would be a dramatic change in the pattern of visiting.

To Susi it seemed somewhat rich that the Reverend should continue to dictate the terms of their relationship in this way. Indeed he might have done better to count himself fortunate that his long years of abuse had not been drawn to the attention of either his bishop or the law. Yet if he had already come to this realization, as was probable, it had not prevented him from repeatedly seeking to vent his wrath at the rejection he felt. Maybe he deserved to be punished for the failures of the past, he conceded, but was he obliged to witness the suffering of Irene Mann too?

I would like to express my sheer disgust at the fact of there being no [Christmas] gift for mother either this year or last. Yes, I can understand your attitude to *me*. As far as I am concerned you have probably done the right thing. But mother? What has she done? The woman who has saved your life, and thereby given you every single thing you have – why should she suffer? By all means jump on me, do your damnedest if you want to, but leave my wife alone.

Then, shortly after New Year 1988, it was Irene Mann's turn to write. It was true that she had been quietly suffering while her husband blustered, but now she had decided to break her silence. Forgetting that she had chosen to look the other way while her foster daughter was the subject of repeated abuse at the hands of her husband, she too had decided to give Susi a piece of her mind:

> Christmas Day and Boxing Day were, as usual, very sad. We had 109 cards sent to us wishing us a happy Christmas. But none of those people know what we know – i.e. that you are all 3 at home together for something like 9 days, and you can't be bothered to come to see us for 48 hours. Why is it that other people do anything in the way of travelling to be with their family at the Christmas holiday time? Whatever sins have we committed more than other people to deserve such treatment? . . .I'm sorry to have to write like this, but does nothing move you? Next Christmas I shall be nearly 82 and Daddy will be 78. What are you waiting for? Our deaths with a will to be read?
>
> In spite of everything, we wish you a happy New Year and send our love.
>
> Mummy and Daddy

Soon afterwards, an already strained relationship deteriorated still further when the Manns learned that their surviving daughter, whose identity and heritage they had done their best to erase, had embarked on a search for her true parentage. On one of her rare visits, Susi summoned up the courage to put them in the picture.

'Oh, by the way,' she said, struggling to master her nervousness and sound nonchalant. ' I've got my birth certificate.'

'Oh, have you?' her father replied.

'Yes, would you like to see it some time?'

'Yes, I would,' the Reverend said. 'I feel as though someone has given me a cold shower,' he muttered as he stooped to pick up his newspaper.

And then, as so often in their soured relationship, the subject was promptly dropped, never to be mentioned again. The dramatic story of Susi's search was not to be shared, even with the people who had played such a crucial role in her survival. The Manns would, in fact, learn of the existence of the Bechhofers in New York, of the late Otto Hald and of his daughter Martina in Leipzig, and of much else besides, but not until several years later, when Sally George's television programme, then still in the making, was broadcast.

At first research for the film seemed not to be making much progress. The BBC team was struggling to gather new facts. Then Susi received a letter from the British Red Cross. It could not have more unhelpful: 'The fate of your mother was unknown. She could have died in an air raid, or anything.'

Fortunately the International Tracing Service at Arolsen had managed to do rather better. As a result of a further, more thorough, inspection of material in their possession, they were able to report that Rosa Bechhöfer had registered with the Labour Office in Munich on 18 January 1936, and that she had been employed as an unskilled worker in the Luitpold chemical-pharmaceutical factory in that city from 17 February 1943 until 3 March the same year. What, wondered Susi, had happened to her during those missing seven years, and, more importantly, after that?

In fact, Rosa had continued to work in one of the few

fields of employment still available to her: domestic service for Munich's better-off German Jewish families – those, that is, who had so far managed to avoid being rounded up. Her two areas of expertise, cooking and sewing, served her well, yet could not prevent the need to change households with unsettling haste, as whole families were carried off. Between 1937 and 1941 she worked for seven employers, as well as doing one month's domestic work at a Jewish old people's home.

During those years, as she scuttled from one household to the next, Rosa found herself working at different times for the Walter, Böhm, Perutz and Bacher families. Unlike the majority of her previous employers, who had been allowed to emigrate if they so wished, these middle-class Jews were engaged in fighting mostly losing battles to gain the right to leave Germany for the United States. In the second half of the 1930s the doors of the Nazi regime were beginning to close, and the outbreak of war had sealed off completely all but the most perilous exit routes. In this respect Rosa was in the same position as her employers, for she had been unable to obtain the necessary permission. Hardly surprising, then, that while preparing meals or darning clothes she would often pause to wonder when she would hear an ominous knock on her door. Rumours were going round the city that it might even come in the dead of night.

As Susi learned of her mother's desperate trail from one family to another, she became very distressed. 'I have an image of someone with a shabby coat on, walking in the wind, with it pressed up to her face, and as she is going around the city from one job to the next, she has an image of we twins fixed firmly in her mind.'

For all the pain that examining the research material caused her, Susi was glad to be associated with the documentary. At last someone was listening to her – a radical departure, she felt, from the past. Naturally she was in no position to compete with the research facilities available to the BBC. Attempting to discover one's own identity, she had long since realized, was a costly business. At the same time she felt confident that if anyone was going to uncover the truth about Rosa, it would be Sally George's team.

Filming was scheduled to begin with a gentle introduction to Germany. Susi was keen to visit Bechhofen, the Bavarian village that was her mother's family's ancestral home.

> Here I found a beautiful cemetery wrapped in an aura of antiquity and charm. The light became perfect as I looked for the Bechhöfers' gravestones – and eventually I spotted my grandparents' headstones. There was a magic and serenity as the sun set on the wild flowers. Then I visited the old grey family house... My imagination caught a glimpse of a young girl sitting on a bench outside...

By contrast, Sally George was pondering darker issues. The question of Susi's sexual abuse was dynamite; even now she could see the headlines in the tabloids: 'Child of Holocaust Abused by Vicar Father' and the like. What worried her was that the shock value of these revelations – which, as serious as they were, touched on only part of Susi's life – would dominate the rest of her story. Indeed, she feared, some people might even be drawn to the film purely out of prurient sexual interest. Sally shared with Susi the conviction that the central theme was the search for identity. However, her objectivity led her to conclude that just as crucial as the dynamic which had eventually triggered Susi's quest was why she had taken so long to embark on it. Behind the whole story lurked the power wielded by a domineering and charismatic man over his daughter. Perhaps more than anything else it was this control that inhibited Susi, as both teenager and adult, from finding out about herself. The Reverend had left her in no doubt at all that if she transferred her affections or tried to pursue her own life in any other way she would forfeit the love and protection without which she felt helpless.

By now Susi herself had realized how she had allowed herself to remain in thrall to her foster father long after she left home and married. She had acknowledged, too, that for all those years she had colluded with him in sustaining an identity which he had shaped and which, if it was blown apart, threatened to deprive him of everything.

For Susi one dramatic effect of discussing the sexual question with Sally was that, although she agreed it should not figure in the film, she now ached to confront her abuser. Old wounds had been reopened, and she at last found the courage to confront her father, if only in writing. She was confident that the Reverend would not dare to deny the accusations, for despite his manifest failures, had he not always remained an honest and God-fearing man? The truth would surely prevail.

'Dear Mr Mann,' Susi wrote, setting a formal tone from the start. How very much more satisfactory to be writing to her father directly, she thought, rather than filling a piece of paper with her feelings about him, only to present it to her therapist, as she had done in the past. She then gave notice to her father that she intended to list his misdemeanours very explicitly. There would be no more games, no more shadow boxing, no more guarded references now. What did the Reverend Mann have to say to these three major charges?

The first was the sexual abuse that started in her childhood and had gone on until she was an adult. What made this even worse was the Reverend's anger, which she had always feared greatly, when his wishes were denied.

Then, rather more difficult to describe but no less real for all that, there was the psychological abuse. What she found particularly difficult to deal with was the Reverend's obsession with her. Not only did he prevent her from forming a proper mother–daughter bond with Irene; he also interfered relentlessly with her attempts to get to know other men, and thus frustrated her chances of forming friendships, let alone a sexual partnership.

Naturally the Reverend had found it easier to drive away her boyfriends when Susi lived under his roof. Once she had left home he had been obliged to change tactics, obsessively telephoning and writing to her, and even turning up on her doorstep without warning. And yet, she now reminded him, after all this he still expected her to behave as a normal daughter and always made her feel guilty when she did not.

The third charge concerned the Reverend's denial of the truth about Susi's true origins: since he knew all about her Jewish heritage, it had been his responsibility to tell her. If he had done so she would have been free to choose which culture to embrace. He had even changed her name, so that she lost everything related to her roots. In short, he should have explained what he had done, and why, when Susi was old enough to make her own choices.

In a final bitter attack Susi added that the Reverend had saved her from Nazi persecution only to become her persecutor himself.

For the former clergyman, fast approaching his eightieth year, the time had come for confession. It was long overdue, but, never before challenged, he had never before confessed.

The Reverend's reply began with an admission that he had trembled on reading his daughter's words, and that he felt justly humiliated and dirty. He conceded that she had a right to make her accusations. Why should she carry burdens which were not of her making? he asked.

Then, in an eloquent confession of guilt, he wondered why he had not been 'blown off the face of the earth'. Having just delivered himself of this anguished cry, somewhat contradictorily he set about justifying his treatment of Susi. He had had no 'motives', he explained; it was just that when she was a child he was fascinated with her beyond reason. He came to adore and ultimately to be infatuated by her. This was wrong in every possible sense, he confessed, and he alone was responsible for what happened between them. He was exclusively to blame – Susi should be free of guilt and indeed free in every way. At this point he made a tentative plea, repeated later, for his daughter's forgiveness.

The Reverend went on to acknowledge how misguided his possessiveness was, and that this trait was at the root of his problems. Almost from the start he had come to regard Susi as somehow his own, but he could now see this as 'very wicked indeed'.

As to why the Reverend had remained, so hypocritically, in a church whose morality he had betrayed, he could only answer that he had had nowhere else to go. Having failed to find work of another kind, he had remained a preacher for reasons of subsistence if nothing else.

On the question of his erasure of Susi's heritage, he defended himself by saying that she and Eunice had been told the facts of their immediate past when they were only eight years old. It was explained to them that they were not the Manns' own children but that they were adopted. They were always encouraged to have their own Bible – both Old Testament and New – and were never pressed to forget their past. It was true, he admitted, that they were not told the full story, and perhaps that was a grave mistake. However, this was never – he stressed the word – with the intention that they should forget their past: it was because he and his wife did not want the twins to be alienated, hurt by other children or teachers. There was no other reason, he insisted. And as for being Susi's persecutor – and thus being bracketed with the Nazis – it was the very last thing he had wanted to do.

In closing the letter the Reverend spoke of his utter humiliation and of being left with no alternative but to cast himself upon his daughter's mercy and that of the God of both Jewry and Christianity.

Finally the tables had turned. The victim, silent for so many years, had spoken out, had struck back. It had taken her so long to find the courage, but now at last a mirror had been held up to the abuser. For Susi the entire episode was extremely liberating. Suddenly the immense power that her father had held over since her childhood, which had controlled, even crippled her life, began to ebb away.

In fact, Susi felt that she was now the all-powerful one. Could she not inflict yet more damage on her erstwhile tormentor, should she so choose? Certainly there were many moments when she was sorely tempted. She could see now that as long as the abuser holds the power in the relationship, however that power is gained and preserved, he or she is free to continue the abuse. It is only when this power is broken by the abused, like an electric current being switched off, that the abuser's grip is loosened and the power transferred to the victim. For Susi, perhaps more important than the power in itself was the feeling of freedom it brought.

And then came the moment for which everyone helping Susi in her search had been waiting. The public records office in Munich had managed to find out what had happened to Rosa. Hard facts at last, a commodity previously in short supply. The discovery had called for the most painstaking research and now one thing was certain: Rosa Bechhöfer had never set foot on English soil. Frau Schmidt, who had carried out the investigation, was now able to report on precisely what had become of Susi's mother. It was her access to Gestapo records which had done the trick. However, it was not good news.

Frau Schmidt contacted Sally and informed the BBC team, who were filming in Munich, what she had discovered before she told Susi. 'I set Susi up,' Sally now admits.

Although I had heard of Rosa's fate, I simply told Susi that this person 'might be able to tell you something about your mother'. I felt that the film needed to show that Susi really cared. Once again I was rather torn professionally speaking whether or not to include what I knew was going to be a most emotional moment: of Susi finding out about her mother. But what I did not want was to have been faced with filming Susi having revised the emotional process. I wanted raw emotion.

Sally was not disappointed. As Susi's diary records:

There seemed to be an air of mystery surrounding what was to take place that day. I walked into a fairly clinical setting of bookshelves and office material. Frau Schmidt was seated alongside me and I had no idea what she was to reveal. First a picture of the orphanage. I scanned my mind for memories. My mind began to whirl. I thought that all these records had been 'destroyed'. I've lived with this thought all my life and here is my name – with Lotte's clearly written too. I gulp the tears and realize how close I was to Nazi persecution. But here I am instead on this special journey. My hand shakes, lips quiver and I think I will have to leave. Then, in front of me, is a document relating to my father in which the phrases 'ill-health' and 'scratches under the arm' are mentioned. And Rosa has chosen not to disclose her twins. Such pain floods us both. Her denial. I quickly decide she had to do this for our safety. Then I look at the photograph and know I am going to explode. No I can't. Cameras. Sit tight. Clench your fist. Stifle the sob. Feel the pain to the pit of your stomach. Then I say, this is why I am here – to find you. Here you are. But I cannot bear to look at the sadness in your face.

Frau Schmidt continued her explanation, her tone business-like and matter-of-fact. It was clear from her professionalism that she had carried out this role before. She revealed that Rosa's last position as a domestic servant was with the Bachers at their home in Munich's Leopoldstrasse. She was in their employ for some six and a half months, after which she was arrested and taken to a concentration camp for Jews. She spent five months in one camp within the city – originally it had been a monastery, but the Nazis had adapted it for their purposes – before being moved to another at 148 Knorrstrasse.

And then they came to the nub of it all. Frau Schmidt had also found Rosa's name on a list of 343 Jews destined for deportation to Piaski in Poland on 3 April 1942. Not one of these people – man, woman or child – had survived.

'I think she was the victim of a mass shooting,' Frau Schmidt said quietly. 'And I think that was the end of Rosa Bechhöfer.'

On hearing this, Susi recalls:

> I began to shake and sob. I had a picture of this person fleeing for protection, to be finally caught and my worst fear was realized. Then a voice at my shoulder said: 'You knew that this was what you might find.' But there can now be nothing worse than this. This is the worst moment of my life. All these thoughts whizz by in my mind. It is worse than a horror movie. I long to escape. I want to scream and scream... I rush out. But there is nowhere to go. Sally follows. I sense her concern. I screech out: 'Oh God, and he destroyed Rosa's trust.' Once again EJM's shadow was there.

The following morning Susi realized that she might be able to effect her escape after all, if somewhat belatedly. Overwhelmed by her experience of the previous day, she set off in search of a travel agency in the centre of Munich to book an earlier flight home. She longed for the stability, the everyday ordinariness and familiarity of her home town.

Over the past twenty-four hours Susi had undergone an extraordinary experience. Having spent half a century knowing nothing at all about her mother, she had found Rosa, only to lose her again just as suddenly. But at least now the process of mourning could begin, she consoled herself. All along Susi's mission had been to know. And now she knew. She knew too that such knowledge brought but one thing – immense pain.

Shortly after New Year 1991 the documentary 'Whatever Happened to Susi?' was broadcast on BBC2. The 'raw emotion' Sally had wanted was in ample supply, and undoubtedly accounted for the programme's enthusiastic reception. But not every letter was complimentary. Although the names of the Reverend and his wife had been changed in the documentary to Hopkins, this had not prevented the elderly couple from being identified with great ease as Edward and Irene Mann. And not just in the United Kingdom, where the programme was first shown, but later in a number of other countries. This was hardly surprising, for the couple's faces could be seen in close-up several times in the film.

Many eloquent words were written in defence of the Manns, a common objection being that they had been maligned, and that in particular the Reverend was a highly respected member of the Baptist Church and, although a fundamentalist, was by no means the 'hellfire and damnation' preacher he had been portrayed as. It was also stated with conviction that he and his wife had always placed the children's interests before other considerations, and that the overprotectiveness of which they had been accused was in fact genuine care.

For such support the Manns showed not the least sign of gratitude, although perhaps encouraged by it, they went on the attack, anxious to present themselves as the aggrieved party, the innocent and unwitting victims of abuse at the hands of the media. Irene Mann explains:

> When we saw the film we just felt as if somebody was walking over us. There wasn't a single word of appreciation that the twins had been rescued. We were upset about this, because we had made Eunice and Grace our lives. Then we thought that other people have suffered and that we too must be prepared to face this. But I must say that I was very interested to see all the people Grace had met, and of how she had managed to go about doing this. My husband's reaction was one of despair.

He just became silent. And for us both, there was nothing we could do or say about it. It was a fait accompli. We just felt at the mercy of the film. We threw ourselves upon the mercy of the public. But we shall never be able to get over the hurt of having been kept in the dark over the whole affair.

It was after Susi's meeting with Frau Schmidt and the completion of filming in Munich that a new twist in Rosa's story emerged. Susi would have been happy to accept the researcher's version of events and let the matter rest there, had she not seen one particular letter.

Aunt Martha, Rosa's elder sister, who had managed to emigrate to America before the war, had already revealed that she had an important document in her possession. It was a letter written in 1946 by one Maria Forster, with whom Rosa had worked in domestic service. Fearful that she might be arrested at any time, Rosa had asked her colleague to contact the New York Bechhofers on her behalf should that fateful day arrive, and entrusted her with various documents. Maria had given Rosa her word that she would do so at the first opportunity, and this she did.

20.6.46

Dear Sir/Madam

Since it is possible to write with America, I will fill a commission of your sister Rosel Bechhöfer to inform you that she was a cook by Miss Heines, Bauerstrasse 22, where I came as a domestic servant. After more processions she came into a concentration camp. Then she became ill – breast operation – and must go away 1943 with a transport, unknown where. I never heard from her anything more. It was very painful for Rosel. I enclose this birth certificate she gave me to keep it. So take this information to further use. I am able to give you more information in case you need them.

Respectfully

Maria Forster

No reply came from New York. Evidently a black sheep Rosa would remain, even in death. But that unbending attitude was not what most concerned Susi now. The simple fact was that the information given by Maria did not square with that provided by Frau Schmidt.

If Rosa had been shot in 1942, why should Maria state without hesitation that she was sent to a concentration camp the following year? And had not the Central British Fund for World Jewish Relief reported that she had applied to come to England during the spring of 1943? Furthermore, the International Tracing Service had recently uncovered new evidence of Rosa's having worked in a factory during the first part of that same year. While Susi was in no doubt that her mother had died at the hands of the Nazis, she was left with the painful feeling that some crucial information was still lacking. For this reason her file on Rosa, weighty though it was, could not be closed with a clear conscience.

It was fortunate for Susi that Frau Schmidt, herself of Jewish stock, was equally determined to establish the truth. An archivist by training, she too had a horror of loose ends, especially those relating to the Holocaust. After delving once more into Gestapo records she was eventually able to shed new light on the question of Rosa's fate.

Dear Susi

I am writing to tell you that just yesterday I have found a pile of Jewish passports in Nazi police records. Among these was your mother's, Rosa. All the passports in the sack (exactly 50) belonged to people who were deported to Auschwitz on 3 March 1943.

So it seems that Rosa was quite definitely put down for the transport to Piaski in April 1942, as I told you earlier, but got seriously ill with breast cancer and then was sent to hospital, and unfortunately Auschwitz later. The last camp in Munich was still the one in Knorrstrasse. Now the Maria Forster letter makes sense to me.

My best wishes to you

Finally, then, the truth. Rosa Bechhöfer had perished at the most notorious of all the Nazi death camps: Auschwitz. The very name made Susi's blood run cold. Rosa had at last been found. But at Auschwitz, alas.

'I opened this letter,' Susi wrote in her diary, 'and once again I felt my whole inside collapse.'

> For here it said that that vile centre of extermination had been my mother's final destination. And yet somehow I had known all along, however much I might have protested to the contrary. But I have this strong image, which I now cannot get out of my head. It is of Rosa walking towards her death. As she is confronted with the gas chambers, with all the people naked and crammed in together, all the time she is thinking to herself – 'I did what I could, I did what I could for my twins.' And that her final prayer would have been for Lotte and me – 'may God save my beautiful daughters.' And to you, my darling mother Rosa, who I was to be with for so very little in this life, I say just one thing: that I have missed you and longed for you all my life. More than you will ever know. May your soul now rest in peace.

As the days went by, Susi thought too of the letters of sympathy, mostly from complete strangers, which had arrived after the showing of her story on television. One that particularly touched her, with its reference to her mother, was from Maureen Goldberg in Leeds:

> I am writing to tell you that all my family watched '40 Minutes' last week and we all felt very deeply for you. You have been in my thoughts ever since.
>
> I feel immense sadness for your dearest mother, Rosa. I know that she would have been extremely proud of you.
>
> Shalom

ELEVEN

Susi: A New Identity

For many people their middle years are a period of security and stability; gone are the uncertainty and impetuousness of youth. Not so for Susi Stocken. The dramatic outcome of her search for her identity and her parents' fate has obliged her to grapple with problems of a very fundamental nature.

Alan Stocken, who witnessed each stage of the process, if not every detail, nowadays occasionally makes light of his wife's metamorphosis, teasing people with a riddle. How could he possibly have started out, he asks, by marrying Grace, only to now find himself wed to Susi without there having been a divorce, a formal separation or any indeed any change of partner in between? It is a good line for broaching a difficult subject with new acquaintances. But, although the passage of time has taught Susi to smile along with everyone else, her journey of discovery was no laughing matter. There were many times when she paused to wonder whether she would ever adjust to so much trauma and change. A few years on, however, she has only one regret.

'I just wish that I had initiated everything much earlier,' she admits. 'So in a sense I feel that I have to make up for lost time. The most wonderful thing is for that dark cloud of not knowing to have gone. That was desperately important for me. And Susi is now a person in her own right, which I feel is a basic principle of human survival.'

In fact, attempting to dispense with Grace was the one part of the quest which, far from being painful, was a real pleasure. For Grace had been a thoroughly unhappy person, downcast, isolated and depressed, for very many years. However, while to those around her it might have looked as though Susi had killed off Grace, Susi herself does not see it in that way. To her it feels that she has retained and integrated Grace's capacity for caring, in such a way as to make Susi much stronger, much less of a victim.

Central to changing one's identity is the issue of names. While Susi had no difficulty at all in reclaiming the name given to her by her mother at birth, for those watching her search from the sidelines matters were not quite so clear-cut. 'I find it very difficult to accept that she is now Susi,' admits the Reverend Mann. Sometimes I call her "dear" because I don't quite know what to say. So I no longer call her Grace. But nor do I call her Susi.'

Irene Mann has been equally confused. At the head of her letters she continued to use the name she and her husband had given to Susi, but, instead of closing it with the Manns' customary 'Ma and Pa' she seemed suddenly to lose her resolve, signing off with 'as ever, both of us'. Sometimes the situation was evidently so sensitive that even this compromise would not do, with the result that letters to Susi and Alan would open 'Dear Both' and close 'From us both'.

At that time it was only first names which were at issue. The effect was nothing like the disruption caused by Susi's decision to jettison her married surname. No longer a Stocken, she henceforth wished to be known as Susi Bechhöfer, the name which appeared on her birth certificate. It was a decision that was frowned upon and even derided by some family members and friends. 'Since making the change back to Bechhöfer,' Susi explains, 'I now feel able to embrace the name which was blotted out so long ago and in so doing more easily accept my German–Jewish heritage. As part of the reintegration of my personality I have had to reclaim Susi Bechhöfer.'

Notifying banks and building societies of a change of name is not a particularly onerous task; nor is changing it officially by deed poll a complex or costly procedure. But could the thoroughly English and Christian persona of Grace Stocken be obliterated with just a few strokes of the pen? In fact, edging towards Judaism seemed to Susi to be a natural step, for she was simply reaffirming the faith she had been forced to abandon nearly fifty years earlier. Yet happy as they were about her decision, it did not prevent members of her newly discovered orthodox Jewish family in New York repeatedly voicing their concern.

'Because we continue to be what we are,' explained Jerry Bechhofer, 'whilst she has to deal with being someone else.' Susi sought to reassure her transatlantic relatives that they should have no worries on her behalf. And for a while she seemed committed to learning about the beliefs and practices of orthodox Judaism. Proud of her rediscovered Jewishness, she found out all she could about the faith into which she had born but which had been denied to her from her infancy. As in other areas of her life, she felt the need to make up for lost time.

And it was not all abstract theology. Wishing to become more familiar with both Jewish prayer and ritual, Susi attended a number of synagogue services. Rabbi Jeffrey Cohen of Stanmore Synagogue devoted his whole Seder service during the spring of 1989 to her story, aware of its symbolic power. 'It did not feel at all strange to me,' Susi noted in her diary, proud, as a practising Christian, to have been able to accommodate this transition. Nor did the Jewish tradition of lighting a memorial candle, in this instance on the anniversary of her mother's death, strike her as out of place. On the contrary, this kind of ceremony was where religions met and was an appropriate way to remember and honour Rosa Bechhöfer.

Yet for all her initial enthusiasm Susi soon realized that she would have difficulty in embracing Judaism in its entirety. There was no disputing that she was being welcomed into the fold, but at times the invitation to acknowledge her Jewishness felt distinctly proprietorial, and she recoiled at what seemed like a claim being made on her soul. There was also the hard fact that, living in Rugby – a town Jerry Bechhofer had characterized as not exactly a thriving centre of Jewish life – she could not suddenly become Jewish in a practical, everyday sense. No local framework existed of the kind that bound together the American Bechhofers, and indeed the orthodox-Jewish culture as exists in England remained alien to her. For this reason she would henceforth adopt a pragmatic approach: taking pride in being born Jewish while in daily life remaining a practising Christian. Her Christian roots, she decided, tugged too strongly at her soul to allow her to return the commitment the Jewish community would without doubt require of her.

Maybe it is because Frederick Stocken's own roots have had less time to establish themselves; or maybe he has a more open mind than his mother. Whatever the case, he soon found himself taking a long, hard look at Judaism from both a theological and a philosophical perspective. At first this came as a surprise to Susi, because her son had never been enthusiastic about her quest and had denied any interest in her family's Jewishness or even the fate of her mother. In time, though, this changed. Free of the pressure of his studies, he began to reflect on how his mother's discoveries might impinge upon him. The simple fact was, if she was a Jewess, then he must be a Jew.

Nowadays Frederick can admit that being Jewish means a lot to him. But, like Susi, he stresses that he remains Christian and therefore goes to an Anglican church. At the same time his faith has not prevented him from wanting to find out all he can about the Judaism. Indeed being Jewish has served to deepen his understanding of Christian experience. To illustrate this, Frederick cites Thomas Cranmer's 'Evening Prayer' of 1552, which begins with the Priest saying: 'O Lord, open Thou our lips', to which the congregation responds: 'And our mouth shall shed forth thy praise.' On discovering that those same words also start one of the Jewish services, albeit in Hebrew, he realized that Cranmer had borrowed from something the Jews had been saying for five thousand years.

Frederick sees his mother as more interested in the blood link that her Jewishness entails than in such questions of faith and tradition. By contrast, for him the most pressing question is: how do you cope when you straddle two major world religions?

In truth, Susi has struggled to bridge this gap and embrace the Jewish faith. But in an area less complex than the matters of the soul she is the first to admit that she is authentically Jewish. For her features are unmistakably both Semitic and East European, as Jerry Bechhofer was quick to point out after seeing a photograph of her before her visit.

> When your letter arrived with the striking picture of a young woman I said to my wife: 'How did she get this picture of her mother?' And then I realized it is not a photo of Tante Rosel but of you. You look exactly like your mother as I remember her. You have what is called in German a 'Mishpocho-face'. The word 'Mishpocho' is of course a Hebrew word. It means FAMILY. What a wonderful thing!

Susi's reunion with the Bechhofers and reaffirmation of her Jewishness had its repercussions not just on her immediate family but, inevitably, on her foster parents too. As Irene Mann pointed out:

> I can understand that she is happy to meet the Bechhofers, but she forgets that they left both the twins and their own mother to fend for themselves. That does rather annoy me. And if anyone might be thinking of pointing the finger at either my husband or me for not having sufficiently nurtured their Jewish heritage, then let them be reminded that they also happened to be half Aryan too.

Susi does not try to conceal the non-Jewish side of her parentage, what she sees as her German roots. Even before she began her search she had always felt at home in that country and had an immediate emotional response to hearing the German language. But if being both German and Jewish is hard enough, how much more problematic for an English-woman brought up in a strict branch of the Christian faith.

> My Germanness seems to irritate some people. But I don't apologize for it all. Germany did carry out the Holocaust. Not all Germans were responsible for that though. And I certainly wasn't. So I don't feel that I need to reject my German roots at all. I was denied being a German for many years, just as I was denied my Jewish roots. Now this has been given back to me. In fact I feel rather privileged in that I can now choose how much of the culture I wish to take on board and assimilate.

Susi's friendship with Brigitte Hald, a key figure in her quest, remains strong. 'It's wonderful to have this bond,' says Brigitte. 'I'm so grateful, as a German living in the period immediately after the Holocaust, to have been able to help someone who was so dreadfully damaged by the Nazi regime.'

And Alan Stocken, of course, has stood by his wife through it all. Even when his surname was given its marching orders he accepted it as another part of the complex pattern of adjustment and integration that Susi had started and had to complete. She could not have hoped for a more understanding partner. As far as Alan is concerned, it doesn't matter if Susi is German and Jewish, or Christian and English. He is in no doubt that for Susi the most important outcome of her quest has been the discovery of an identity of which she had long been deprived. For him, it has been enough to see his wife emerge from those difficult years with a new sense of direction.

On 25 February 1989 thirty lone twins gathered at Queen Charlotte's and Chelsea Hospital in London. For all but one of them, it was the first time they had knowingly met another lone twin. The participants were divided into three groups: those who had lost a twin at or around their time of birth; those whose twin had died in childhood; and those who had lost a twin in adult life. It was an opportunity for the survivors to examine together the profound and unique sense of loss caused by the death of a twin, and to find ways of coping more easily with the pain.

Those attending the meeting that day formed the Lone Twin Network, an organization in which Susi is now actively involved. She joined because for many years she had steadfastly refused to examine the crushing pain caused by the death of Lotte/Eunice, a denial bound up with her attempt to survive by distancing herself from distressing feelings. Like Susi's former identity, that pretence has fallen away. Even so, she is the first to acknowledge that, having started so late, her mourning of her sister is far from over.

Four months later another group of people assembled in London for a special celebration: the fiftieth anniversary of the Kindertransport. People had flown in from all over the world to attend, among them a good number of VIPs. Bertha Leverton had worked herself up into a fine state of anxiety, having scarcely slept in the forty-eight hours preceding the opening of the reunion. Nevertheless she summoned up the energy warmly to welcome those who, as children, had

shared the same frightening experience half a century earlier.
'Hello, Kinder,' she called out from the podium, and at once
the hall was filled with a sense of togetherness.

Yet for Susi the experience was somewhat different:

> Even there I was like a lost soul. Because it appeared to me as
> if everybody else at least had their Jewishness to fall back on.
> And there was me, with my very English and Christian up-
> bringing. They all seemed to know who they were, whereas I
> had only just begun to find out about my identity. The cantor
> sang beautifully in Hebrew, remembering our parents and
> loved ones whom we had left behind. There was hardly a dry
> eye between us.

Religion proved to be the one area where Grace might be
said to have reasserted herself, because eventually, for all her
dalliance with Judaism, Susi decided that:

> I can't sit on the fence any longer. I loved the truths taught to
> me as a child, both at Clarendon and at home: that there was a
> person called Jesus, who simply loved me enough to go to the
> cross. I now feel the need to return to these beliefs, Jewish
> though I am. Because the church is one of the few places
> where I can and do experience a sense of belonging. It has
> become clear to me that God is the only answer. How can I
> accept anything other than the message of the Gospel?

One viewer who wrote to the BBC some time after its
screening of Sally George's documentary was of special
significance to Susi, as clearly Susi was to her. She was very
old and apologized for waiting so long before putting pen to
paper. Her name was Miss Grace Weston. Almost forty years
had passed since the two Graces had last been in touch.
Miss Weston had not been at all surprised to learn from the
film that Grace Elizabeth Mann, her former pupil at
Clarendon School, was now Susi Bechhöfer. For it was she
who had first drawn the fact to the attention of the teenage
schoolgirl. Now, so many years after sowing the seeds of a

momentous quest in young Grace's mind, she offered some timely and heartfelt advice. 'Just remember all your foster parents did for you,' she urged, mercifully oblivious of what Susi had suffered at the hands of her foster father, 'and thank them any time you have an opportunity. Leave the rest to God, Susi, and with His help try not to be bitter.'

Inevitably, there continued to be many times when Susi felt great bitterness, for she had been abused and her whole life overshadowed by a stifling possessiveness against which she felt powerless. When, all these years later, she had finally discovered that her mother had ended her days in Auschwitz, she felt as if she had been violated all over again.

It often sent a shiver down Susi's spine to think that she had escaped from the horrors of the Holocaust by a hair's breadth, and she was haunted by the thought of those children from the Antonienheim who were never to join a Kindertransport. Most haunting of all was the image of Rosa being herded into the gas chamber and, amid a struggling mass of defenceless humanity, being overcome by noxious fumes. And Rosa Bechhöfer was but one of two million to die in that hell.

In Susi's mind there persisted an indissoluble link between her mother's fate and her own. For had her mother not been abused too, in the vilest imaginable way? And she herself had wanted to lash out, to inflict harm, to exact revenge on the Reverend Mann whenever and wherever an opportunity arose. Yet here was Miss Weston, well-intentioned but ignorant of the facts, like so many others before her, urging her to be grateful. Let the Reverend be grateful, Susi seethed: grateful that he had never been reported to the police.

True, it helped to confront her father as she eventually did, yet it could not at one stroke exorcise all the years of anger. Susi had a lot more pain to go through – for anger is always painful – before she achieved the radical shift in perspective that she had by now realized was unavoidable. The key lay in taking power over her own life:

> I came to the conclusion that I no longer wished to remain a victim for ever. I also realized that I had to take a measure of responsibility for my own behaviour too; that it's just not good enough to attribute anything and everything that might not have worked out in your life to another person. I think because of all the other things that were going on in the home, though, it has taken a long time to appreciate that his was also the hand that fed and clothed me, and that opening their door to us twins was an extraordinarily noble thing to do. It's all too easy to look the other way when confronted with suffering. But the Manns chose not to. I have also been helped in this process of reconciliation by my adoptive father's unambiguous acknowledgement of what he did to me. And I have come to sense his very real sorrow and shame. So I have finally been able and willing to offer the hand of peace and forgiveness. And as I did so I wondered why I had wasted so many years being angry with him, hurting myself in the process too. Why had I not done this a long time before?

'We went into a lot of detail when we met recently,' explained the Reverend Mann, 'as a result of which she said two very significant things. Firstly that she wanted to put the past behind us. And, more important still, I finally heard the words that I had been hoping to hear for a good many years, "I forgive you." My heart gave one huge leap.'

After so many painful years – years of denial, of anger, of rebuffing contact – Susi had at last acquired the strength to extend the hand of forgiveness, and to understand its value. And yet making her peace with the man who had brought her suffering along with the stability she now acknowledged, had by no means been the most significant achievement for Susi.

> The most important piece of the whole jigsaw was to have found out the truth about my mother, and in so doing about myself. Even though what I found was more horrific than

anything I had ever imagined. In my life that remains I will always have her in my heart. So how can I feel anything other than delight that I went on that voyage of discovery? Because at least now I know who I am.